Amazon.com #1 bestselling book to speaking in the US and Canada to creating hundreds of videos together) all start with a simple idea that is then added to over and over again. Ideas, connections, action - all vital for success.

And that's what Ken McArthur does through his jvAlert Live programs. And I speak from experience, having been there, meeting people like Ken, Frank Sousa, Stefanie Hartman, Daven Michaels, Jane Mark and Phil Basten, and JoAnna Brandi.

Can one person's actions or ideas impact millions? Absolutely, as you'll find throughout this book. Here's to Ken and all he does to impact the rest of us!"
~ **Charlie Seymour Jr,** Video-Crazed MBA Marketer
CreateYourOwnLegendNow.com

I0088901

The Impact Factor: How Small Actions Change the World

## Love Notes

*Acclaim for Ken McArthur's The Impact Factor:*
*How Small Actions Change the World*

"Skip this one at your own risk! Best-Selling Author, Ken McArthur's "The Impact Factor" is a master stroke of simple ideas that deliver remarkable results! Everyone has an impact whether they want to or not, but YOUR impact will be so much greater if you put the brilliant insights that Ken reveals into immediate action! Grab this book and your world of impact will explode!"
~ **Rick Frishman,** Founder of Planned Television Arts

"When I had the blessing of appearing on the ABC Hit TV Show, Secret Millionaire, I saw first-hand how small actions change the world. If you're ready to make a positive difference in the lives of others and have a greater positive impact, then read and absorb the ideas in this brilliant book by my friend Ken McArthur! He's a man who comes from the heart and truly cares about making a difference!"
~ **James Malinchak,** Featured on ABC's Hit TV Show, "Secret Millionaire" The World's #1 Speaker Trainer™ Founder, www.BigMoneySpeaker.com

"You make a difference. In this highly inspirational book, Ken will show you how your actions, your words and your behavior impact your friends, your family and the planet in a positive way. It will lift you up and help you connect to yourself and your passion like never before."
~ **Stephanie Frank,** Best Selling Author of The Accidental Millionaire

"Scintillating storytelling… backed by science. An all too rare combination. Bestselling Author Ken McArthur's "The Impact Factor" reveals how small actions really matter if you want to reach

the masses with your ideas, products or services. And best of all, Ken's unique take on impact helps you cut through the clutter and get people's attention in a noisy world. This book is a must-read for any entrepreneur, or anyone who wants to be one. I personally know Ken and have experienced first-hand the impact he has on people like YOU. It's a virtuous circle indeed."
~ **Mike Morgan,** Million Dollar Copywriter

"Can one person really matter in the world? Ken McArthur says 'yes, you can'. Through strong storytelling, Ken connects the dots to show you how your words, actions and choices make a difference – not just to others, but to your own success. But Ken doesn't sugar-coat it: sometimes the choices we make, and events outside our control, have a negative impact. Still, if you feel like you're not having impact, if you're not creating the success you want, this book will give you a huge boost by listening to how other people's stories and being inspired by them to keep reaching for success, connections and meaning in your life. As Ken says, 'If you want life to come up "heads" and all you get is "tails," you need to keep flipping the coin.'

"But inspiring stories aren't enough to get you into action. So Ken has included practical advice as well, from marketing to mindset. In simple, digestible chunks, he outlines for you the steps you need to take to set goals, find your target audience and connect with them to have impact. Ah, but if we could only stop sabotaging our best efforts, wouldn't that be great? Ken covers that, too. This book will give you the motivation and the skills to continue taking action -- the best actions possible -- on your dreams."
~ **Karyn Greenstreet,** Passion For Business

"Ken McArthur is Truly Making a Difference! If there is a phrase that sums up Ken McArthur it is the Big Positive Impact he is making in life. Ken made a decision to live his life that way, but

what I love is he observed that making an impact wasn't an option. He saw good or bad, big or small, you make an impact. And he took it upon himself to enlighten us on how each of our actions can equal a positive change."
~ **Tracy Repchuk**, International Speaker and Best Selling Author of 31 Days to Millionaire Marketing Miracles

"Everyone wants to have an impact. Few know how, or even believe it's possible in today's crowded world. Ken McArthur shows you how you are already having a major impact, whether you do anything or not, in "The Impact Factor: How Small Actions Change the World." In the book, Ken makes an undeniable case proving that the tiniest of events can and do have major impact, then he shows you some spectacularly small changes in your thinking that can so easily change your current impact into a major positive force that can easily travel the world and change it as we know it."

"Skip this book if you want. You'll continue having a tremendous impact on the world, either way. But, that impact might not be the one you want, if you do skip it. I hope you choose to dive in! There's no one on Earth I trust more than Ken McArthur to gently, lovingly, blow your skull right off the back of your head with the verifiable reality of how truly tiny your steps to greatness can be.
~ **Alan R. Bechtold,** best-selling author of "Will Work for Fun: 3 Simple Steps for Turning Any Hobby Or Interest Into Cash" (John Wiley and Sons), editor and publisher

"If you really want to make an impact on the people around you, or around the world, Ken McArthur's book, "The Impact Factor," is the place to start. In it, Ken explains how everything we do has an effect, and gives you real world tips on how to make that effect positive, and make it huge. I've watched the impact Ken has had on people in the years since we first met. He knows what he's talking

about, and he says it in a way that makes it usable and effective. Best kind of training, from the best kind of trainer."
~ **Paul Myers,** TalkBiz

"Ken McArthur's "The Impact Factor" reveals heart bending stories of real people making a difference, combined with the crucial art, science and technology of today, to reveal how YOU can have more impact, reach the masses and make a difference."
~ **Joel Bauer,** Author, Mentor & Perceptionist

"Most of us go through life never realizing the impact we make on the people and the world around us. Ken eloquently brings this impact to light and shows us our infinite potential to be the light that is so needed today. This book is timely, relevant and needed."
~ **Daven Michaels,** CEO, 123 Employee

"Being successful in life means making connections that matter. Ken's philosophy, detailed in his book, "The Impact Factor" tells you why Ken matters to so many people, and how you can, too."
~ **Stephanie Diamond**

"If you've been lying down, staring at the ceiling, and trying to figure out how to make something of your life, get up long enough to grab a copy of The Impact Factor. The writing may be simple, but the content is deep. It'll get you up and moving, and before long, changing the world."
~ **Shel Horowitz,** bestselling author of eight books including Guerrilla Marketing Goes Green.

"Ken McArthur is incredibly passionate about providing value and impact through his teaching. Ken is a true inspiration and a mentor who was instrumental to my company's success. I remember the first event I attended hosted by Ken. Not only did Ken devote valuable time in providing guidance; he laid out strategies that

reshaped my thought process. I recommend that everyone learn the steps he has outlined in his new book. These very powerful steps can impact your business success"
~ **Andy Huang,** AimVenture.com

"If you want your message to be heard and make a difference, The Impact Factor will teach you how, and inspire you to do so. Ken McArthur's message is both educational and highly motivating... A must-read for anyone thinking of starting something that will truly make a difference."
~ **George Levy,** BreakthroughDigitalMarketing.com

"Ken McArthur is one of those people you just love to connect with and thank your lucky stars when you do. If you have been fortunate enough to be at any one of the many events Ken hosts, you know exactly what I am talking about. Ken makes an Impact wherever he is and with whomever he interacts. His books are brilliant not only because Ken is brilliant, but because he is also genuine and generous. He big-heartedly shares his brilliance and his humanity and encourages you to do the same. If you want to have a bit of Ken with you at all times, then I highly recommend buying The Impact Factor: How Small Actions Change the World. Read it, use it and see how your actions can change the world."
~ **Sue Guiher,** Founder/CEO, Thrive for Success, Author, Speaker, Small Business Marketing Expert and Coach

"Well, having known Ken for years, and having gone to his JV alerts a half a dozen times, at times travelling 10,000 miles just to be impacted by his caring attitude, whether him saying who do you want me to introduce you to, to small details such as is the room temperature too cold. It is funny, I'm involved in many prayer groups and I always make sure to tell the groups that we don't realize how small insignificant actions can impact other people's lives, and for others those small acts of kindness can change their

lives whether it is a kind word, a smile, or a positive attitude. As a professor and entrepreneur I always remind myself what one of my students told me 10 years after she took a marketing class with me: "Sir, I only remember you telling me ' If you dream it you can achieve it'- Walt Disney". I never thought that sentence would impact her so much, yet she started a sizeable company based on those words. Read this book and take small actions that will impact your micro as well as your macroenvironment. The only thing I have to say is that I wish I had written this book, but I'm glad it impacted my life."
**~ Bob Debbas**

"Having worked for Encyclopedia Britannica, I know from having read "The Great Books" that a Great Book does not need an endorsement, and neither does Ken McArthur's, "The Impact Factor". So what's my excuse for Highly Recommending this book? It's really quite simple, The Impact Factor, so clearly opens up your Eyes, your Awareness and your HEART to the one small idea that so many Unhappy people are truly missing. The idea that most people, because of ignorance and a spirit of perfection, fail in a BIG way to do something small because they CAN'T SEE the Future Result of how their little thing can make a HUGE difference. This is the same little blind spot that almost caused me to commit Suicide. I hope you read the book and don't miss this one small point. Just remember this simple quote, 'NEVER underestimate the day of small beginnings'. KEEP SMILING...I love you", Deremiah *CPE.- Deremiah *CPE, Inspirational Speaking Star, Author of "52 Great Weeks" and Nightingale Conant Life Time Achievement Award, Winner of the "Acres of Diamonds". The 16 year old boy who overcame Suicide and LIVED to tell about it.

" 'That idea was not in this room when we walked in,' is one of my favorite sayings, born out of working to build several businesses with my business partner, entrepreneurial psychologist Dr. Marc Kossmann. Everything we've done (from creating our

# The Impact Factor:

# How Small Actions Change the World

## By Ken McArthur
## with Ronda Del Boccio

Action Plan **Publishing**

The Impact Factor: How Small Actions Change the World

# Dedication

To Miro Grudzinski,
for his demonstration of what true passion is.

The Impact Factor: How Small Actions Change the World

## Table of Contents

The Prequel – "A Conversation with Seth Godin"        15

Introduction – "The Truth"        21

Chapter 1 – "Chaos"        29

Chapter 2 – "Three Guys on a Couch"        37

Chapter 3 – "We Can't Afford It"        41

Chapter 4 – "Randomness"        51

Chapter 5 – "Infinite Impact"        59

Chapter 6 – "Because I Miss Dany"        73

Chapter 7 – "Creating Advocates"        77

Chapter 8 – "Passion"        85

Chapter 9 – "Is Your Best Stuff Still On the Drawing Board?"        95

Chapter 10 – "Taking Action"        97

Chapter 11 – "Measured Results"        101

Chapter 12 – "Creative Ideas"        103

Chapter 13 – "Finding Your Audience"        111

Chapter 14 – "Your Social Network"        123

Chapter 15 – "You have to Like People!"        125

Chapter 16 – "Systems"        135

Chapter 17 – "The Mental Criteria Necessary for Success"        145

Chapter 18 – "Growth"        161

Chapter 19 – "Paying Your Way"        163

Chapter 20 – "The 'What Can I Get' Level"        167

Chapter 21 – "The Five Stages of Change"        171

Chapter 22 – "Something Has To Give"        173

Chapter 23 – "The Pareto Principle"        179

Chapter 24 - "Life is Hard, Then You Die"        183

Chapter 25 – "Life is an Adventure"        189

Chapter 26 – "Now it's up to YOU!"        193

The Sequel: "The Impact Manifesto"        197

Acknowledgements        199

About The Author        201

Resources                                           205
Name Index                                          207

# The Prequel:

## "A Conversation with Seth Godin"

In preparation for this book, I had a conversation with Seth Godin, the best-selling author of *Linchpin*, *Tribes*, *The Dip*, *All Marketers are Liars*, *The Purple Cow*, and so many other bestsellers that have changed the way business people think and act. He's the most influential business blogger in the world. He's the founder and CEO of Squidoo.com, and a very popular speaker. Listen to the stories he has to tell.

KEN MCARTHUR: Thanks for doing this. The thesis of my book is we all make a difference, whether we want to or not. If you do nothing you still have an impact in the world. You can think of the example of a mother. They have a huge impact on that child even if they do absolutely nothing, but not only that, they have an impact on everybody that child comes into contact with, and that impact spreads from person to person to person.

Small actions cause amazing impact. As a matter of fact, I think probably the most impactful thing that I've come across is the simple kind word that somebody gives to somebody, so I think that small actions really do make a difference.

The reason we think our actions don't make a difference is because we don't measure our results. We measure our checkbook every day. It goes up and it goes down, and when it goes down we start kicking in our actions and we start doing things to make sure the balance goes up.

But, we don't really measure our impact in the world and if we did, I think we might do things differently.

SETH GODIN: First, I want to congratulate you for doing this hard work. I think it's important, and I'm glad someone's doing it, and I'm glad that you've chosen to invest your time on speculation to make something happen. So thank you.

KEN MCARTHUR: Well, thank you very much.

SETH GODIN: Six years ago I was flying on United from Springfield to Chicago and the person in front of me in line checking in to the flight said to the person at the ticket counter, "I need to check-in for my flight to Chicago. I'm flying first-class and blah, blah, blah." And, this person was probably 70 years old. It was a woman and she was with her son and the person behind the counter said, "Thanks very much, but this is a small plane and you're in seat 7." And, the woman starts freaking, jumping up and down basically yelling, "I have to fly first-class. I've got claustrophobia. This is impossible. That's not what they told me when I booked the ticket." And, the woman behind the counter said, "I understand. I'm sorry if they didn't give you the right advice, but this is a commuter plane." And the woman is just vibrating with anxiety. And the woman behind the counter said, "Don't worry Ma'am. All the seats on this plane are first-class." And, she said it with kindness and authority and the woman instantly calmed down and the rest of her trip was saved, because it's true all the seats were the same and if you want to call them first-class, they were first-class.

The second story I'll tell you about occurred at a place where a lot of important things happened for me, which is a summer camp up in Canada called Arowhon, and this was some work I was doing with a twelve year old girl.

What I did for a living up there was that I taught canoeing. A canoe is a seventeen foot long, wooden vehicle, much bigger than any teen has ever piloted in their life, and the idea that you can get in it by yourself, tilt it way over to the side and pilot it like a native American in circles and do other cool things in it is pretty amazing.

And, the interaction that I had with this girl who was angry all the time and impatient and had a temper and wasn't good at interacting with the world when the world didn't line up the way she wanted it to was … I spent a half an hour with her, helping her think about her posture and her breathing and the way she was interacting with the physical world around her, and it was the first time that anyone had ever apparently spent that much time, one on one, telling her she was doing something right, and the act of just taking a little bit of extra time to give her the confidence to maneuver through the world ended up changing not just her physical posture, but her interactions with the rest of the world forever. I mean, that was the last time that she ever fought with anybody, the last time that she ever punched anybody in the face.

And, I think about that interaction often, because it would have been very easy for me to just say, "Well, I got a hundred and eighty other people I need to work with." But, something in that moment told me that a little bit of extra time on my part might have a big impact for her.

KEN MCARTHUR: Isn't that incredible, because that's what we've found over and over again. It is those moments that really change lives, and so many times people don't even know that they had that impact.

SETH GODIN: I think that's the key part of it, at least for me, that most of the time I would rather not know. If you're doing it to have an impact you're going to burn out because you put in all this effort, and even if it works 35% of the time, that means that the truth is most of the time, and so you're getting all this feedback that it's not working most of the time.

There are very few things that we are happy to do that fail two-thirds of the time. Imagine if you went to take a shower and two-thirds of the time the water didn't come out. So I'd rather be generous for generosity's sake, not because I'm doing someone a favor, not because I'm looking for a response.

And that's something you learn from writing a book. You put it out there in the world. You have no idea what a difference it makes. Sometimes you hear someone say a year later, "Oh yeah, because you wrote this, I did that," but that's not why you do it.

KEN MCARTHUR: It's funny, I had a speaker at one of my events who was sitting there talking about these concepts with me and I was telling her what I was doing and she said, "Well, I quit talking about Internet marketing because of the fact that I just didn't feel like it was making a difference."

And within two seconds, a young woman came up to her and said, "I have to tell you that you changed my life ten years ago because of the fact that you were out there doing this stuff." And it was just incredible, because it was within seconds, and that's pretty amazing.

SETH GODIN: Love that! I hope those two stories helped you at two ends of the spectrum.

KEN MCARTHUR: That was perfect, as I should know, and thank you for that. And here's a gift for you. You've impacted my life, and I'll keep taking small actions to make sure that your impact on me spreads beyond my life.

SETH GODIN: Perfect! I love that.

# Introduction

## "The Truth"

Imagine a teenager, the son of a Presbyterian minister in a one stoplight Colorado town. His hair is cut close – the barber tells him he can never grow long hair because his is too thick and unruly – he has the thin, gawky, semi-pimply look of every teenage boy that you never wanted to be.

It's a lazy Sunday afternoon and he's lying on his bed in an upstairs bedroom of a house built long ago as a manse, probably occupied by a long line of pioneer ministers out in the wilds of the Southwest. Now it's the breeding place of more ideas than one teenage boy can handle.

He looks across the room at the old dining room table, which he convinced his parents he needs, because any normal desk was never big enough to hold his ideas.

His eyes drift to the ham radio he uses to eavesdrop on the rest of the world.

As his eyes follow the antenna out of the window to the tree in the yard, his mind drifts in and out of focus as he wonders if there is anything he really knows is true.

Great ideas tend to come when you have no boundaries on your thinking. They're scary because great ideas are — by definition — not normal. They're different than run of the mill variety ideas. They just click.

That teenage boy was me.

So, is it just a coincidence, when I contemplate the big questions of life, I keep thinking back to my teenage years?

Probably not.

In my teens no dreams existed which were beyond my reach, or problems too great to solve.

I started with a clean slate.

As a teen, nothing seemed above challenging. So I challenged everything.

What is the truth, and does it have many faces? Is it unknowable?

I began to doubt everything.

What if the world was nothing like I imagined it to be?

Did the world even exist? After all, dreams can seem as real as our daytime world.

Was there a God? How could I possibly know for sure? Was there anything which was undeniably true?

So I started from a blank slate and attempted to find something I knew to be absolutely true, and found almost nothing. In the unbounded and unconquered mind of a teenage boy there are no limits.

- There might not be a God.
- I might not be a person.
- Other people might not exist.
- The world might not exist.
- Good might not be good.
- Bad might not be bad.

- One might not equal one.

It was pretty radical thinking for a teenage kid – or maybe completely common.

In fact, in all of my mental wandering that day, I only discovered one thing I was sure of beyond a doubt.

My single point of undisputed truth was this simple idea – I existed.

I was relieved in later years to discover I wasn't the only person who thought this way.

Rene Descartes's first wrote "Je pense donc je suis," ("I think therefore I am") in his Discourse on Method in 1637.

The Discourse on the Method is a philosophical and mathematical treatise that is one of the most influential works in the history of modern science. Descartes' method gave a solid platform from which all modern natural sciences could evolve.

Descartes started his line of reasoning by doubting everything, so he could assess the world from a fresh perspective, clear of preconceived notions, and he too came down to the same clear truth I accepted on a lazy Sunday afternoon.

I exist.

I can't prove YOU exist (only you can do that), but if you are thinking about what I just said, then you exist too – and we have a connection.

Connections are what this book is about.

They start small and have huge impact.

Without connections, we can't have impact. With them we can have unimaginable impact.

Eventually, we are forced to move beyond what we know to the things we perceive as having truth. And when we make that move, people try to put limitations on our beliefs.

In my early science classes, my teachers told me electrons, protons and neutrons were about as small as things got, and the known universe was only as big as science allowed.

Even at my young age – or maybe because of it – I dreamed there were things bigger and smaller than science imagined.

The truth science claims today is beyond imagination, but even with what science imagines in this instant, we find some pretty remarkable numbers.

The number of atoms in the entire observable universe is estimated to be within the range of $10^{78}$ to $10^{82}$

An average human body has approximately 7*1027 atoms. That is, 7 followed by 27 zeros:

7,000,000,000,000,000,000,000,000,000.

99.999999999999% of an atom's volume is just empty space, and only about 0.0000000000000000000042 percent of the universe contains any matter.

The universe is pretty empty – and you are too.

Even more remarkable, all atoms are connected by forces that exert influence across infinite distances.

When you start imagining yourself at the atomic level as a mass of extremely small electrons, protons, and neutrons all swirling around in a space that is comparably empty, you realize you aren't much different than the known universe.

You are made up of exactly the same stuff, and whether you are looking at galaxies or atoms, the same forces are at work.

Take a look at a model of a hydrogen atom, and then compare that to earth's relationship to the moon. There's a size difference, but think for a moment about the similarities.

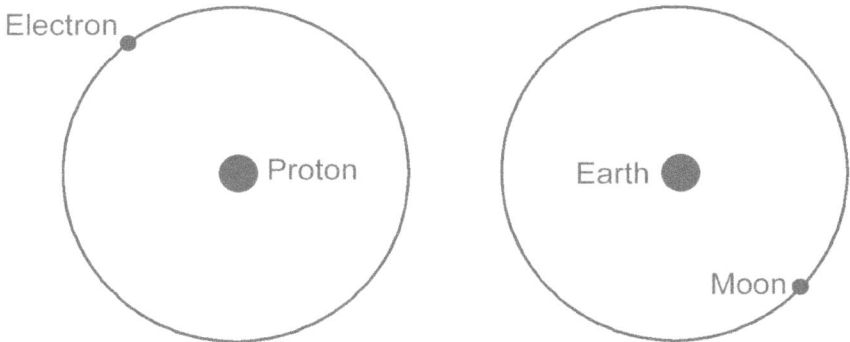

What is the universe made of, and what holds it together?

Science tells us that everything that goes on in the universe can be accounted for by one of four forces. In order of strength they are:

- The Strong Force
- Electromagnetism
- The Weak Force
- Gravity

As it turns out, the strength of each force is inversely related to the distance it reaches.

The strong force acts over a short distance, while gravity acts over a large distance. Gravity, the weakest of the four forces, is about $10^{-36}$ times the strength of the strong force.

If it's a dry day, you can rub a comb across your shirt to generate static electricity, and then hold it over a piece of paper resting on a table. With the right set of conditions, you can lift the piece of paper right off the table despite the fact it takes an entire planet to keep the paper on the table because of the force of gravity.

The force of gravity, which keeps the universe together, is easily overcome by a tiny electromagnetic force, but the range of gravity is infinite. Every object in the universe exerts a gravitational force on everything else.

On the other hand, the strong force – the strongest force in the universe – is practically unobservable at distances greater than 10 femtometers, which is approximately the width of the average nucleus of an atom.

All connections have their strengths and weaknesses. Proximity is a huge factor in influence.

If you aren't feeling strong enough to change the world, think about gravity. The weakest of all the forces in the universe moves galaxies.

Or if you feel you are too small to make a difference, imagine how small the range of influence the strong force has. It can't change anything beyond a single nucleus, but it is the glue that holds everything together.

It turns out that small forces make this universe possible, and small actions change the world. The question is, "what about you?"

The universe is ahead of you, and the possibilities unimaginable.

You will discover how you can spark your ideas, start your adventure, select your strategy, supersize your results and survive what the world throws at you. But first comes the chaos!

# Chapter 1

## "Chaos"

There are over 6,830,586,985 people in the world according to the U.S. Census Bureau's International Database, and you may be tempted to think that one person can't have much of an impact.

Of course, intellectually we know the truth.

Someone makes a difference.

Can one person have an impact? Absolutely! People do it all the time.

But what are the chances that you will?

It turns out we know exactly what your chances are of having an impact.

Here's how one person accidentally figured out what your odds are of having an impact, made a difference himself, and then passed it on to you.

Ed loved the outdoors. He hiked the White Mountains of New Hampshire, smelling the tickling scent of evergreens and alpine flowers on a mountain breeze

An active hiker and cross-country skier, Ed accidentally changed the world when he brought about one of the most dramatic changes in mankind's view of nature since Sir Isaac Newton.

Ed's insights influenced a wide variety of both scientific and nonscientific applications, including the geometry of snowflakes, computer generated music, and how to predict which movies will become blockbusters, but he was a shy, unassuming man.

A friend said he was like a mountain goat and knew every trail in the White Mountains and the Rockies. Despite his quiet nature, he had a surprising sense of humor, and for someone who changed the world, a very humble spirit.

Ed had an interest in math, so he studied at Dartmouth College in the town of Hanover in western New Hampshire and went to Harvard, where he got his master's degree in 1940. But the war effort moved him to the United States Army Air Corps in 1942.

In the Air Corps, Ed used his mathematical skills to help with weather forecasting. Eager to know more, he ended up getting a second master's degree in meteorology from the Massachusetts Institute of Technology. After World War II ended, he continued to study and was awarded his doctorate in 1948.

He worked as a meteorologist for MIT and published major works, and became full Professor of Meteorology and the department head.

It was heady stuff. Ed was a well-educated man.

Despite all of his studies, it was a simple accident in 1961 that produced the results that led to the insights which brought him worldwide fame.

In the course of his studies, Ed developed 12 differential equations that worked together to create models of atmospheric conditions.

He wasn't trying to predict the weather. He was trying to figure out what would take place if certain atmospheric conditions existed.

Ed was using a simple digital computer, a Royal McBee LGP-30 to run his weather simulation.

The LGP-30 was inexpensive – by the standards of the day – a drum-memory computer with a retail price of $47,000.

The LGP-30 was commonly referred to as a desk computer. It was 26 inches deep, 33 inches high, and 44 inches long, not including the typewriter shelf.

The computer weighed about 740 pounds and was designed by Stan Frankel, a Manhattan Project veteran and one of the first programmers of ENIAC.

The single address instruction set had only 16 commands, and the only printing output was the Flexowriter printer, which was a modified typewriter, working at 10 characters per second.

The results of Ed's calculations were printed out to an accuracy of three decimal places on long reams of printer paper. The process took hours.

Having obtained results from running his program, he decided that he would like to carry the calculations further.

Instead of starting the program from the beginning – which would have taken hours to return to the point at which he stopped the calculations – Ed started the program in the middle of the calculations by inputting the data as calculated by the computer at a particular point in the original run of the program.

Returning after having a cup of coffee, Ed came back to check the calculations and was surprised to see that the computer had come up with a completely different range of answers than the original calculations.

At first, he thought it must be something wrong with the computer, because software should always come up with the same answers, given the same data.

Eventually Ed ruled out hardware problems and discovered the different results were caused by a difference between the precision that the computer stored the information, and the three digit precision of the printout that he inputted the second run's starting data from.

The computer stored the numbers to six decimal places in its memory. To save paper, Ed only had it print out three decimal places. In the original sequence, the number was .506127, but he only entered the first three digits, .506.

The data had not been printed out to the same number of decimal places as the machine had stored, so the initial data was slightly different for the second run – it was different in the fourth decimal place.

By the standards of the time, it should have worked.

Ed should have gotten a result very close to the original numbers. After all, most scientists don't expect to get measurements with accuracy to three decimal places. Since it's impossible to measure using most common methods, the difference shouldn't have much of an effect on the results.

Ed proved this idea wrong, all because he needed to understand how a tiny change in the initial data could have such a major effect on the calculations.

That's how Ed Lorenz discovered chaos.

But he was not the first.

Jules Henri Poincaré discovered chaos in the 1880s while studying the three body problem proposed by Isaac Newton, who defined and studied the problem of the movements of three massive bodies – the

Earth, Moon and Sun — which are subject to co-dependent gravitational attractions.

The problem gained special fame for its great difficulty and became popularly known as the three-body problem.

Poincaré realized that at least a major part of the problem in lunar theory consisted in evaluating the perturbing effect of the Sun on the motion of the Moon around the Earth, but the calculations were tedious without the aid of computers, and Poincaré's discovery had not led to any significant developments.

The simple LGP-30 computer offered a tool to take the calculations to a new level. When Lorenz understood the significance of his discovery, he wrote it up in the paper 'Deterministic Nonperiodic Flow'.

The abstract starts out:

"For those systems with bounded solutions, it is found that nonperiodic solutions are ordinarily unstable with respect to small modifications, so that slightly differing initial states can evolve into considerably different states. Systems with bounded solutions are shown to possess bounded numerical solutions."

In other words, small changes have such a big impact that it makes it impossible to predict the results over an extended time period.

Ed Lorenz's paper, like Poincaré's work, had little impact when it appeared, but it has become one of the most quoted papers of all time.

The set of equations and the attractors described by them have become famous as the 'Lorenz equations' and 'Lorenz attractors', respectively.

A meteorologist remarked that if the theory was correct, "one flap of a seagull's wings could change the course of weather forever."

Apparently, the idea of a single butterfly having a far-reaching ripple effect over time appears first in a 1952 short story by Ray Bradbury about time travel (*"Sound of Thunder"*). Ed started using the more poetic replacement of "butterfly" for the seagull. When he failed to come up with a title for a talk he was scheduled to give to the American Association for the Advancement of Science, Philip Merilees came up with, "Does the flap of a butterfly's wings in Brazil set off a tornado in Texas?"

The picture of the butterfly flapping its wings and the effect of the tornado stuck, although as the metaphor spread, the location of the butterfly and the location of the tornado varied widely.

The metaphor speaks to the idea that a butterfly's wings could create minute changes in the atmosphere which might over time create or alter the path of a tornado in a given location.

In other words, the tiny flap of a wing changes the initial condition of the atmosphere, which causes a chain of events leading to large-scale changes of events.

If the butterfly didn't flap its wing, the results would have been drastically different. And without a single flap, the tornado would not have happened.

This effect came to be known as the Butterfly Effect. The difference in the starting points of the calculations is so small that it is comparable to a butterfly flapping its wings.

This phenomenon is called "sensitive dependence on initial conditions."

Just one small change in the initial conditions can have a huge impact.

Just like we are confident that what we do doesn't make much difference when there are over 7 billion people in the world, Edward Lorenz didn't expect the fourth and fifth decimal points to matter much.

Such a small amount of difference might be called experimental noise, background noise, or an inaccuracy of the equipment. Even in a perfect laboratory, you can't expect that much precision.

If you start with 2.000001 instead of 2, the final result can be entirely different.

It's impossible to get accuracy at that precision. Try measuring the length of a city block to one millionth of an inch and see how that works out.

Ed eventually decided that it was impossible to predict the weather accurately over a period of time much longer than a week, but his accidental discovery put him on the path to other discoveries that eventually came to be known as Chaos Theory.

So we start with chaos. Any action can have an immeasurable impact, and it's the small actions that make a difference. You can make a difference, too.

# Chapter 2

## "Three Guys on a Couch"

Although this story has become known as the famous, "Three Guys on a Couch" story, the couch really wasn't big enough for three guys. It was actually two guys sitting on the couch and one plopped in a chair.

It all started because I didn't get out much.

I'd been working on the Internet since there was an Internet, and I'd had some pretty good success stories. Armed with a technical background, when the Internet boom took off, I knew my way around. I started building web sites for clients who knew they needed to be on the Internet but had no clue why. Over time, I developed software platforms to make development easier, and started using the software to build my own successful Internet ventures.

My first big success story was a joint venture with Jim Daniels, an early pioneer in the Internet "work at home" space, and it brought in almost a quarter million dollars of recurring revenues in the first six months. With the success of one joint venture, I started looking at ways to find more joint venture partners, and I developed a website for Internet marketers to partner together. This site attracted some of the top marketers in the world.

On the first day of pre-launch, my new site, jvAlert.com, was ranked as #362 out of all the sites on the Internet by Alexa.com, so I was having a great time.

Although I was working with thousands of people, most of my days were spent in a windowless basement office working alone. As I said, I didn't get out much.

Don't get me wrong, I love my alone time, but I also love being with other people. There's something about seeing people face to face no amount of online contact can ever replace.

Luckily, I was invited to lunch with some Internet marketers in the Philadelphia area.

What a joy! Frank Garon, Andy Jenkins and Mike Merz were there, and we had a great time talking about all of the things that would bore most people to tears.

It was a blast, so I decided to see if other people in the area might like have lunch. If only a few responded, we could have another great time together. As it turned out, Frank Sousa emailed me from Spokane, Washington and told me he would like to come, and Jane Mark and Phil Basten wanted to come down from New York City, and there were a couple dozen more, so I decided I needed to do a little more than lunch.

The very first JV Alert Live event attracted about 30 people and was planned for a single day. Since Frank was flying across the country, we decided to get together for a networking dinner the night before the event, and to have a networking breakfast the day after the event before Frank flew back to Spokane.

There were no speakers. We decided to do simple "Hot Seats." Each person in the group who was working on a project made a short presentation of what they were working on and the entire group tried to help them fine tune their ideas.

It was a great time and many of the friendships forged have continued since that day.

After the event, Frank Sousa, Sterling Valentine and I sat in the lobby and talked.

It was a simple conversation. It was the kind of conversation people hold at every live event I've ever participated in. "What do you want to do next?", "What should I be doing?", "How can I do that?"

I was thrilled by how well my first event had gone, and wanted to do more events. Sterling wanted to finish and launch a product, and Frank shared his wisdom and awesome heart.

The exchange was nothing special, but out of a single conversation, millions of dollars were made, thousands of lives changed, and lives were saved. Frank Sousa's life changed, for sure.

The Impact Factor: How Small Actions Change the World

# Chapter 3
## "We Can't Afford It"

The phrase Frank Sousa remembers most from his childhood is, "We can't afford it." Frank's father drove a laundry truck and didn't make a lot of money. There were eight kids in his family, and although his father was very loving and supportive, the words kept ringing in Frank's ears, "We can't afford it. We can't afford it."

Frank had been interested in electronics since he was about twelve years old and his record player broke. Frank took it over to his neighbor, a Boeing engineer with an electronics shop in his basement, who had the latest vacuum tubes, capacitors and resistors. The neighbor troubleshot the problem, handed Frank a soldering iron and a capacitor and said, "Here, you need to replace this."

Frank did it and was hooked.

He started to learn electronics in high school and in his junior year acted as an assistant to the teacher because he knew more about electronics than the teacher did.

At age seventeen, when he got out of high school, Frank joined the Coast Guard as an electronics technician. It was a memorable experience for a young man and included a year and a half long tour to Italy. After his service ended, Frank went to work in the shipyards building Navy ships.

One cold drizzly January day, in Seattle, Frank was perched on a yardarm, six inches in diameter, lying on the cold steel trying to hook up a radio antenna with freezing rain beating against him. He was 150 feet up in the air and thinking, "I don't want to do this for the rest of my life."

About that time, Frank learned of a multi-level marketing program, called "Success Motivation Institute." Their product was a briefcase full of cassette tapes which promised that if you listened to the tapes, you would become rich and famous.

Frank was 22 years old and married to the woman he calls "the most incredible woman in the world." He immediately quit his job. His plan was to find lots of people, get them motivated, sell them cassette tapes and make everyone lots of money. The only problem was, at 22 years old Frank didn't know too much about motivation or making people money. He didn't sell a single one briefcase, and went totally broke.

It became something of a pattern in Frank's life. Frank tried a number of different MLM programs without much success, but nothing stopped Frank cold. Because of this experience, he learned to heed the old sage advice, "Don't quit your day job." Frank got another job, moved to Spokane and started rebuilding his life.

His first job was to manage a team of technicians who installed and serviced teller machines by banks around the country. Then he took another job with a company who developed handheld meter readers for electric companies where he built a service department. For a time, his department's team were the "golden boys."

But then one day they called Frank in and out of the blue told him they didn't need him anymore, and they had already terminated his entire department.

Frank had been working hard, putting in twelve hours a day at the job. When he arrived home at 2:30 in the afternoon and opened the door, the first thing his wife asked him was, "What did they do? Kick you out?"

You can imagine how Frank felt.

In tears, Frank vowed never to let anybody do that to him again. To this day, he never has.

In so many circumstances, we allow one person or a single organization to control the outcome of our life. We let go of our future and cede control to another person or group of people.

Frank says, "We are taught from the time we go to kindergarten to respond to bells." A bell rings; we come in and sit down at our desk. Another bell rings and it's time to go out to recess. Another bell rings and it's time to eat lunch. We go through our whole life that way. When we get to high school, the bell rings and it's time to go to history class. All of this prepares us to go to college, learn and get a good job.

For the rest of your life you are someone else's slave. If they decide they don't need your department anymore, you are out the door. That doesn't mean going into business is the best thing for everyone, but for Frank it seemed like the answer.

Frank started a computer repair business and he did something right this time. He sat down with a marketing professor at a local junior college and told him he was out of work and wanted to start a computer store. Frank asked the professor how to do market research.

The professor gave him a lot of ideas. He suggested Frank visit other computer stores, see what they were selling, how much it cost to get into the business, and to talk to the owners to find out what their problems were. Frank quickly found out Spokane needed another computer store like he needed another hole in his head. What Spokane really needed was someone who could fix computers. Frank was just the guy to do that, and so he was successful!

So what did Frank do with his newfound success? He decided to sell his business and try another MLM program. Why? Frank thinks it was probably boredom. I call it, "bright shiny object syndrome."

As Frank was trying to build his MLM organization, he found he was getting pretty good at recruiting people over the Internet, but the people he recruited didn't seem to be able to do the same thing. Frank went broke again.

Then it dawned on him that he could help other companies do "search engine optimization." Search engine optimization (SEO) is the process of improving the visibility of a website or a web page in search engines via the "natural" or un-paid ("organic" or "algorithmic") search results. Back then SEO was brand new.

Frank had just started to pick up a few customers when his youngest son Joe, a youth leader at their church, asked him cook for about 160 kids at a youth summer camp. Frank wanted to help, but was just starting to get some business and he really needed the money badly. So he decided to lug two computers up to the camp. He ran a telephone wire to the cabin and thought he was all set, but cooking for 160 kids is pretty much a six in the morning until midnight proposition and by the third day, Frank was sitting on his bed in tears, praying. He had come to the summer camp to serve God, but he just couldn't do it all, so he told God, "The business is your problem and I'm not turning these computers on for the rest of the week", and he didn't.

When he got home the next Monday, the telephone rang and it was the second largest gift basket company in the country. They had a website built for them and in the past year had only one sale. They were a huge company with a huge mailing list, but still weren't able to make more than one sale. The gift basket company had heard about what Frank did and wanted to know if he could help them.

Frank could help. As a result, there wasn't a month that went by for years when Frank didn't earn four to five thousand dollars in revenue from that single call.

The same week, Frank got a call from one of his competitors who said, "Frank, you've been kicking my butt all over the Internet. I just tied together a contract with a big software company who wants to send us business. If I could guarantee you $10,000 a month, would you come and work with me?"

When you are flat broke and someone comes along and offers you $10,000 a month, what are you going to do? Frank thought really hard for about two or three seconds, and his business really began to take off.

As the business developed, Frank brought in more and more employees to help and grew to a million dollar business, but Frank never really liked having employees. He's a big fan of Robert Allen's phrase, "No hablo employees." So Frank backed off and asked the question, "Why don't I do what my customers are doing." Frank could see what his customers were doing and they were making a lot of money, so he started selling affiliate products, got rid of his employees, and the company ended up being Frank and his two sons.

Frank was a part of Affiliate Showcase, and then joined jvAlert. When he got the e-mail from me about jvAlert members getting together for lunch, Frank immediately responded, "I want to come." Since the very first JV Alert Live event, and participating in the now famous "three guys on a couch" incident, Frank said he would never miss an event – and he never has.

I loved the chance to spend time with other people. and after the success of the first event, I wanted to keep doing live events.

Soon Frank was asked to speak at a jvAlert Live event in Philadelphia. While there Frank met Mike Koenigs, who was speaking about video production. They got to talking at a networking dinner at Dave and Busters on the second night of the event.

Mike was telling Frank about all of the exciting things he was doing with video. Mike would make three- to four-minute videos and put them up on YouTube.com, and he had a list of 30 to 35 places where he would submit videos. By posting these videos, Mike was able to get on the first page of Google listings almost immediately.

Frank was getting excited about Mike's results, but Mike was complaining that it was taking so long to submit the videos to the various websites. Frank thought about that problem for a minute and said, "Why don't we build a program where we can send the video over to a server and we'll let the server send it out."

Mike thought that sounded good, so they laid out their plan, literally on the back of a napkin. Frank went back home to Spokane and after about six weeks and a $600 investment, Frank and Mike had a prototype of what would become Traffic Geyser.

When they started, the new application just took videos and submitted them to the various websites, but then they decided to split out the audio portion and make podcasts from the audios. Then they took the audios, had them transcribed, and set them out as articles to article directories.

Their idea, which started on the back of a napkin, grew and grew until it was a multi-million dollar company. At that point Frank had a decent amount of money coming in. He had never seen that kind of money before. In fact, before he had gone to jvAlert Live, he had set a goal to double his income, but after this single joint venture he was able to increase his income more than tenfold.

Frank was the technical guy for the new company. He designed the backend servers and set up the entire system, but he felt like he was getting to an age where his brain just wasn't as fast and sharp as it used to be. As time went on, he felt like he was getting to the point where he didn't feel that he could serve the company as effectively as he wanted.

Eventually, Frank approached Mike about buying him out, which they did, in a multi-million dollar buyout.

There are key decision points in life. Frank, realizing that he didn't want to be stuck on a freezing yardarm for the rest of his life, made him aware of a choice. He could have decided that life is hard and you just have to tough it out, but he didn't.

Frank says that what he should have done was to go out and build a sideline business first, and then quit his job. After failing in his network marketing attempts, when he pursued a dream of owning a computer store, he made a crucial choice to do some research before jumping in. Frank says he "... finally decided to do things the right way, and that made all the difference in the world. We were successful."

Frank stays on top of what is happening in the world and what the needs and wants of the people are. He realizes that what he thinks the world wants might not be what the world thinks it wants.

As Frank says, "You have to find out what people want, what people are buying, how they buy it, and offer it to them."

He has impacted countless people since that first jvAlert Live and his success with Traffic Geyser. Many people count riches in possessions, but Frank counts his riches in the ability to help other people.

For example, Frank's brother-in-law and his wife Sarah had a heart for foster children. Over time, they had fostered over 30 children. When he suddenly died, Sarah was left with seven foster kids in the house at the time ranging from a year old to twenty-three years old. The only money coming in was the small income the state gave her for taking care of the foster children.

Because of his success, Frank was able to buy a house for Sarah and the children and give them a safe place to live where he could be nearby to help out when they had problems. Of course, Frank being Frank, he loved the kids. Frank says he collects daughters, and people around the world are feeling the love he gives out.

Frank says those are the kinds of things you can do when you build your business, and to Frank that means so much more than driving a big fancy car.

So many times it's the little things that make a difference. If your carburetor goes out, it may be no big deal, but for some people it could be life and death. One thing breaks and then you've lost your transportation, or your job, or … well, the list goes on.

Frank says that when a friend needs a couple thousand dollars, he can now choose to hand them the money. And Frank can take the time to help. He can travel anywhere in the country to help someone in need. Frank says, "It's all about freedom, and it's not only the freedom to give your money, it's the freedom to be able to give your time."

When we are in desperation mode it's easy to think about giving up on helping other people when you have so many problems of your own. To have the freedom to be able to make choices, and to think of other people first, is a powerful thing.

Frank met John Di Lemme at a jvAlert Live event. Frank says, "he was talking about millionaires this and millionaires that." John is a powerful speaker, but after his talk Frank went up and introduced himself and said, "You know, it's not all about money." Frank says, "He kinda shook his finger at me and said, 'Don't give me that crap. My wife and I just gave a hundred thousand dollars to a crisis pregnancy clinic." That made Frank think.

A year or so later, Frank had a picture in his mind of his church. Their kitchen was way too small. Behind the kitchen was a storage area. Frank laid out a plan and said, "If we move this wall out and put a doorway here, then we can put a convection oven over here and we can put a stock pot stove over here and a triple sink over here." Frank laid everything out and sat down with the elders of his church and presented his plan to them. The elders were looking at him with glazed eyes as Frank made his presentation until Frank said, "… and I'd like to pay for it." That changed the perspective. The elders approved the plan.

That night, Frank was sitting down at his table writing the biggest check that he'd ever written. As he was writing out that check, he thought about John and tears started streaming down his face. Frank called John on the telephone, forgetting that he was on the East Coast, got him out of bed and reminded John of the time that he told him the story of how he was finally able to write his own check.

I imagine that story meant a lot to John, and I know it meant a lot to Frank. It's the small things that count. The freedom and choices you can make when you get a chance to take control of your life. When you get the opportunity to think about what you really want to accomplish in your lifetime, you realize that life is so short.

When he was 22 years old, Frank had a conversation with himself and said, "Self. What do you want to do with your life?" His self came back and answered, "I'm not sure, but I want to help people." Now Frank says he's living his dream.

Frank tells people they need to create their own economy. On his wall Frank has a Bible passage: "Whatever you do, work at it with all your heart, working for the Lord, not for men." Colossians 3:23. It's Frank's life verse.

Frank grew up hearing the words, "I can't afford it. I can't afford it." But, there were some other words which Frank's father used to recite from a poem that still echoes from those days, and goes deep into Frank's heart. Many years later Frank discovered that the words were written by the poet, Edgar Albert Guest.

*Somebody said that it couldn't be done,*
*But he with a chuckle replied*
*That "maybe it couldn't," but he would be one*
*Who wouldn't say so till he'd tried.*
*So he buckled right in with the trace of a grin*
*On his face. If he worried he hid it.*
*He started to sing as he tackled the thing*
*That couldn't be done, and he did it.*

# Chapter 4

## "Randomness"

*How we misunderstand the significance of everything we do.*

If I hadn't gone to lunch with a few friends, my life might have been entirely different. I would never have met Frank Sousa, the three guys would never have spent time together on that couch, and jvAlert Live would never exist, which means that Sterling Valentine wouldn't have gone on to make over $100,000.00 in 92 days, and Frank Sousa and Mike Koenigs would not have met. If they hadn't met, Traffic Geyser wouldn't have been born, which led to a countless stream of events and products which have impacted thousands of people's lives, who have in turn impacted millions more. Frank could not have built a kitchen for his church or given thousands of dollars to help countless other people.

All gone if I had decided not to make the effort to go to lunch that day.

Leonard Mlodinow tells his father's story in the first chapter of his book, *The Drunkard's Walk: How Randomness Rules Our Lives*:

> "... in Buchenwald, the Nazi concentration camp in which he was imprisoned and starving, he stole a loaf of bread from the bakery. The baker had the Gestapo gather everyone who might have committed the crime and line the suspects up. "Who stole the bread?" the baker asked. When no one answered, he told the guards to shoot the suspects one by one until either they were all dead or someone confessed. My father stepped forward to spare the others. ... Instead of having him killed, though, the baker gave my father a plum job, as his assistant. "A chance event," my father said. "It had nothing to do with

you, but had it happened differently, you would never have been born."

There are so many choices in our life that we can't control.

Randy Manning discovered in a painful way how an event can change the course of someone's life.

> At the age of 28 I decided that I wanted to fly airplanes for a living. I earned various ratings, including my Commercial Rating.
>
> Then the unfortunate thing happened. My mother came down with breast cancer, so she had to quit work. And I had to give up my dream of being a commercial pilot to be with her when she needed me. Between my work and being home to help her, I had a lot of pressure. My mother died at the young age of 63.

Choices can affect us negatively or positively. Here's what would at first seem to be a random event in the life of Cheryl Millett. A piece of graffiti ended up connecting her with her purpose in life and her desire to make a difference.

> I was driving the other day and saw some writing on a concrete wall under a bridge, and for a second, I thought why do people do this? I decided to read the message and it made me smile BIG. This is what it said: "Everyone dies but not everyone lives." I am here to live until I die. I am here to motivate and inspire others to live a life of healthy possibilities!

There are countless choices to make, so how do we choose?

The ways we make choices are influenced by a broad range of factors, including:

- Emotions
- Health
- Hormones
- Personal Experiences
- Brain Structure
- Evolution
- Shared History
- Traditions
- Knowledge
- Logical Processes
- Education

The process of making a decision is so complex that it's difficult to predict what our choices will be in any given situation. In addition, we have limitless options which make prediction almost impossible - just like the flap of the butterfly wings and the weather.

It turns out that even within our own mind we may have different choices coming from different areas of the brain. If you are involved in an accident three times out of every ten times you attempt to drive a car, your "logical" brain will attempt to find patterns in the data, while your "intuitive" side will simply say, "Don't drive a car!"

"Naïve realism" is the doctrine that things are what they seem. Bertrand Russell assures us, "We think that grass is green, that stones are hard, and that snow is cold. But physics assures us that the greenness of grass, the hardness of stones, and the coldness of snow are not the greenness of grass, the hardness of stones and the coldness of snow that we know in our own experience,"

So if things are not as they seem, our options are limitless, our most impactful choices out of our control, and our decision making process is conflicted, what are we to do?

Daniel Kahneman won the Nobel Prize in economics, but his field of expertise is psychology. He spent his childhood years in France and was in Paris when it was occupied by Nazi Germany. Kahneman wrote about an experience he had that explained in part why he entered the world of psychology:

> It must have been late 1941 or early 1942. Jews were required to wear the Star of David and to obey a 6 p.m. curfew. I had gone to play with a Christian friend and had stayed too late. I turned my brown sweater inside out to walk the few blocks home. As I was walking down an empty street, I saw a German soldier approaching. He was wearing the black uniform that I had been told to fear more than others – the one worn by specially recruited SS soldiers. As I came closer to him, trying to walk fast, I noticed that he was looking at me intently. Then he beckoned me over, picked me up, and hugged me. I was terrified that he would notice the star inside my sweater. He was speaking to me with great emotion, in German. When he put me down, he opened his wallet, showed me a picture of a boy, and gave me some money. I went home more certain than ever that my mother was right: people were endlessly complicated and interesting. - Kahneman, D. (2003), "Maps of bounded rationality: A perspective on intuitive judgment and choice," in *Les Prix Nobel 2002* (Noble Prizes 2002), edited by T. Frangmyr.

Kahneman was awarded the Nobel Prize in 2002 for his work on prospect theory, a theory that describes decisions between alternatives that involve risk. It explains how people choose between probable outcomes, and evaluate potential losses and gains.

The biggest challenge that randomness presents is that the consequences of our choices, which are based on random events, are often counterintuitive.

For instance, Kahneman was teaching a group of flight instructors about behavior modification techniques and trying to make the point that rewarding positive behavior works better than punishing bad behavior. One of the flight instructors objected, saying that he often praised people for well executed maneuvers, but the next time they always did worse, and that when he screamed at them for bad results, they got better. All of the other flight instructors agreed and Kahneman had a sense that they were telling the truth.

However, Kahneman was also familiar with experiments which demonstrated that reward works better than punishment. So what is the solution to this apparent paradox? Thinking about the problem, Kahneman realized that the screaming preceded the good results, but didn't cause it.

In any series of random events, an extraordinary event is most likely to be followed – purely by chance – by an ordinary one. This is a phenomenon called "regression toward the mean."

It turns out that all of the student pilots had certain abilities for flying airplanes and that in general they made fairly consistent progress over the course of their flight training. On some occasions, they would do exceptionally well, but those times were mostly the result of chance.

The chances were that following an exceptional performance, the next day's results would be closer to the "mean" (average) results. So when the instructors praised them for wonderful results, chances were the next day would be closer to average performance. But if the student did poorly and the instructor screamed at them, the chances were that the next day the student's performance would be again closer to the "mean" – which in the case of low performance meant they would do better the next day.

It seemed like the screaming was causing good results and praise was causing worse results, but in reality it made no difference at all.

Should we make decisions based on results from acts of randomness? What are the results from believing that screaming at our kids improves their performance?

Maybe a dozen publishers have rejected your book. Does that mean that your book is unsellable? You might feel that way, but it may be possible that publishing is so unpredictable that you may have a bestseller on your hands, and give up long before your perfect publisher sees what you have to offer.

A major portion of success is purely a result of randomness. After all, genius doesn't guarantee success. Knowledge doesn't guarantee success, because as the saying goes, "If knowledge is power, then librarians would rule the world." Money doesn't guarantee success. How many multi-million dollar movies have flopped at the box office? Remember Pets.com?

Based on randomness alone, there will be winners and losers!

If ten people each toss ten coins, the chances are 2 out of three at least one person will come up heads or tails at least 8 times out of the ten – purely on chance.

In poker, your odds of getting a Royal Flush are 649,739 to 1.

Sounds like a long shot, but there are 525,948,766 minutes in a year. So statistically if you are dealt cards at a rate of one per minute, you would get your royal flush within less than 1.3 years.

That's what "hanging in there" gets for you.

Or you could just work twice as fast and get it done in half the time — if you could survive.

That's what "working harder" does for you.

If you team up with 100 of your friends, you can get one deal in 3.65 days.

That's what "joint venturing" does for you.

Any way you work it, I'm convinced, statistically speaking …

*"If you want life to come up "heads" and all you get is "tails," you need to keep flipping the coin."* – Ken McArthur

Eventually, things come up the way you want.

Notice I didn't say, "Wait for things to get better!"

In business, your odds of success are better.

According to U.S Dept. of Commerce, Bureau of the Census, Business Dynamics Statistics …

Seven out of ten new employer firms last at least two years, and about half survive five years. More specifically, according to new Census data, 69 percent of new employer establishments born to new firms in 2000 survived at least two years, and 51 percent survived five or more years. Firms born in 1990 had very similar survival rates. With most firms starting small, 99.8 percent of the new employer establishments were started by small firms. Survival rates were similar across states and major industries.

Compare that to the average length of a job …

Three to five years with jobs held between the ages of 18 and 38 having the shortest duration (America's Dynamic Workforce: 2006; U.S. Department of Labor).

So I'm Statistically Optimistic.

Odds are …

- 4 out of 5 of you will NEVER die of Heart Disease
- 6 out of 7 of you will NEVER die of Cancer
- 22 out of 23 of you will NEVER die of Stroke
- 35 out of 36 of you will NEVER die of Accidental Injury
- 99 out of 100 of you will NEVER die of a Motor Vehicle Accident
- 120 out of 121 of you will NEVER commit suicide
- 324 out of 325 of you will NEVER die as a result of Fire or Smoke
- 1,115 out of 1,116 of you will NEVER die of Natural Forces (heat, cold, storms, quakes, etc.)

And if you keep trying, keep learning and focus on solving real problems …

Odds are you can have your own successful business.

So if you don't like the results you are getting right now – just keep flipping that coin.

# Chapter 5

## "Infinite Impact"

So, one person influences another, who influences another, who influences …

That's the Domino Effect and it's exponential. It's also the way to infinite impact.

Here's an experiment to help you grasp the concept of exponential results:

- Take a sheet of paper
- Fold it in half
- Fold it a second time, and a third time.
- Continue folding -- if you can.

At 7 folds it is as thick as a notebook. At 10 times, it would be as thick as the width of your hand. It can only be done about 12 times, but …

- At 17 folds it would be taller than your average house.
- At 60 folds it has the diameter of the solar system.
- At 100 folds it has the radius of the universe

Just in case you don't believe me, here's the math.

- n $2^{**}$n  km ($0.1^*10^{**}$-6 $*$ $2^{**}$n)
- 0 1 0.1 x $10^{**}$-6
- 1 2 0.2 x $10^{**}$-6
- 2 4 0.4 x $10^{**}$-6
- 3 8 0.8 x $10^{**}$-6  finger nail thickness
- 4 16 1.6 x $10^{**}$-6
- 5 32 3.2 x $10^{**}$-6

- 6 64 6.4 x 10**-6
- 7 128 12.8 x 10**-6  thickness of a notebook
- 8 256 25.6 x 10**-6
- 9 512 51.2 x 10**-6
- 10 1024 0.1 x 10**-3  width of a hand (incl. thumb)
- 11 2048 0.2 x 10**-3
- 12 4096 0.4 x 10**-3  0.4m height of a stool
- 13 8192 0.8 x 10**-3
- 14 16384 1.6 x 10**-3  1.6m: an average person's height (yeah, a short guy)
- 15 32768 3.3 x 10**-3
- 16 65536 6.6 x 10**-3
- 17 131072 13.1 x 10**-3  13m height of a two story house
- 18 262144 26.2 x 10**-3
- 19 524288 52.4 x 10**-3
- 20 1048576 104.9 x 10**-3  quarter of the Sears tower (440m)
- 25 33554432 3.4 x 10**0  past the Matterhorn
- 30 1073741824 107.4 x 10**0  outer limits of the atmosphere
- 35 34359738368 3.4 x 10**3
- 40 1099511627776 109.9 x 10**3
- 45 35184372088832 3.5 x 10**6
- 50 1125899906842624 112.5 x 10**6  ~ distance to the sun (95 million miles)
- 55 36028797018963968 3.6 x 10**9
- 60 1152921504606846976 115.3 x 10**9 size of the solar system?
- 65 36893488147419103232 3.7 x 10**12 one-third of a light year
- 70 1180591620717411303424 118.1 x 10**12 11 light years
- 75 37778931862957161709568 3.8 x 10**15 377 light years
- 80 1208925819614629174706176 120.9 x 10**15 12,000 light years

- 85 38685626227668133590597632 3.9 x 10**18 4x the diameter of our galaxy
- 90 1237940039285380274899124224 123.8 x 10**18 12 million light years
- 95 39614081257132168796771975168 4.0 x 10**21
- 100 1267650600228229401496703205376 126.8 x 10**21 (12 billion light years) approx. radius of the known universe?

Here's the difference between incremental results and exponential ones when it comes to getting new customers.

- Incremental – Add one customer every day and in 30 days you have 30 customers.
- Exponential – Double your customers every day and in 30 days you have 536,870,912 customers.

We all know that exponential results have limits. Just think about the paper you folded. After a while you run into physical restraints and you just can't do it anymore.

The same thing is true if you apply exponential results to a problem like getting more customers. There are limits to markets and getting exponential result may not be easy. Think pyramid schemes if you don't believe that.

But, just like the butterfly flapping its wings, our smallest actions create infinite results.

Maybe the conversation on the couch was purely random, but the results were infinite.

You got a glimpse of how it affected Frank Sousa's life, but Frank wasn't the only person impacted. Every person who came in contact with Frank's changed life was also impacted.

Jeff Wellman was a dairy farmer and his father before him and his grandfather before him and suddenly that became less productive, so he took a job working on a production line in the local baby food factory, running a packing machine.

The company was promising Jeff great things. They were telling him that they were going to move him up in management; they were going to raise his salary, he was going to be able to retire, he would have benefits, he would have everything a wonderful corporate life will give you – then they said, "You're going to be laid off within two years, because this is a union plant and you're at the lowest level of seniority and so we'd really like to keep you … but."

Jeff had a family to take care of including kids with special needs, but he didn't come running to my events eager and eager to get there. In fact, his son Keith had to twist his arm a bit to make him show up at his first event.

Keith knew that his father was in financial trouble and Keith himself had been having some success making a good living on the Internet. So he told his father than he should come to Atlanta to an event that I was doing. He told him to take a look at what we did and see if he thought it might work for him.

So Jeff went to my event called "Get Your Product Done" where I brought in about 30 people to a 3-day workshop to help them get products done that they could sell on the Internet. Jeff was probably hoping that he could just sit in the back of the room and watch and in the process get his son off his case, but that's not exactly the way my events are structured.

We brought in a full video team, photographers, graphic artists, experts, fulfillment services and a professional interviewer to help them create their products, and everyone at the event jumped right in and went to work. In fact, 100 percent of the people at the event walked out with a finished product at the end of the three days.

Some of the attendees took it to an even greater level, and Jeff ended up being one of those people. Jeff put together his product, did a product launch and did $104,000.00 of revenue in 30 days. That changed his life, and the lives of his family.

Ex-Marine that he is, Jeff is an independent kind of guy who's a real action taker. If you get to know him you'll quickly realize that Jeff over delivers on any promise. In fact, he would probably give his right arm for you, and he would be in trouble because of that generosity and sense of responsibility.

Jeff gave like crazy and it didn't happen overnight, but through a solid pattern of taking action, he was able to impact countless people who participated in his membership sites and coaching programs.

He started going to jvAlert Live events and at an event in Long Beach, he brought me up a copy of an e-mail that he had just gotten from a 16-year-old boy. If you were reading that e-mail today you would be in tears.

The boy hadn't had much contact with his father, who was working at a gas station, worried about losing that kind of a position, worried about his future, and he was angry and bitter.

His son showed him Jeff's website, which told Jeff's story from dairy farmer to success. The website had pictures of Jeff's cows on the site. The site explained how Jeff lost his career, was stuck in a job on the production line of a factory and about to be laid off. It revealed how, by creating the product at my event, he had been able to go into work and tell his boss that he wasn't going to be able to lay off Jeff, because Jeff was going to lay off his boss!

The boy told Jeff that his story was inspiring and he wanted to show his father that there was hope. "That could be you, Dad," he told his father. In his e-mail, the boy said, "I don't know if my father will ever do this, but it really doesn't matter, because I know that you've changed my life and that my father now sees that there's some possible value in what I'm trying to do."

And it changed his life, because his father turned to him and gave him the first hug he had ever gotten from his father.

That's the impact that flows from one person, to another, to another – infinitely.

My life was impacted by that chain of events too. JV Alert Live would never have happened the way it did without that conversation. Watching people's lives change at the events impacted me in countless ways.

At each event, I would see more and more lives changing, and finally it impacted me so much that I decided to write my first book, *Impact: How to Get Noticed, Motivate Millions and Make a Difference in a Noisy World.*

In order to prove the concepts that I wrote about in the book, I decided to create a special event in Philadelphia to show that we really could impact millions of people.

That's how I got to tell the story of Deremiah Phillips.

Deremiah was born on the South Side of Chicago. His father was in the Army, and so Deremiah started traveling at the age of 2. By the time he was 12 years old he had lived in 13 states and two cities in Germany, where he lived for 5 years, and in some ways felt like he was more European than American.

Deremiah says he was fortunate because, "My life gave me a tremendous amount of experience in dealing with other people from other cultures." There were plenty of times Deremiah had holes in his pants, but even if his parents weren't able to give him everything he wanted, they always gave him food, a place to sleep and lots of love.

After spending his elementary school years primarily in Germany, Deremiah found himself in Oklahoma, where sports became like a religion to him. It was where he was most comfortable. Sports were where he got his self-esteem.

He lived a very focused, health conscious life because of all of the accolades he received as an athlete.

Oklahoma was a football state, and Deremiah became one of the top running backs in the state, and a starring athlete in every sport he played.

Unfortunately, at the age of 15, Deremiah's parents divorced. This forced him to move away from a very stable, praise-filled environment in Oklahoma.

Deremiah was forced to leave all of his friends without saying goodbye to most of them, and ended up in the ghetto of ghettos on the south side of Chicago.

His mother was on welfare again, and he went from a very good life, back to the poverty level kicking and screaming. It pushed him to the brink. He fell into a deep depression. He was crying every week, hating living in Chicago. He was also dealing with the kids in his new neighborhood who were doing drugs.

Deremiah had gotten a glimpse of what the future could be through his travels and his athletic successes. The kids who surrounded him in the ghetto had no sense of what the future could be.

At the same time, Deremiah had to support his mother on an emotional level. She had suffered from mental illness since he was five years old and had been through a number of nervous breakdowns. It was something that Deremiah wanted to hide; he really didn't want his friends to know that his Mom sometimes talked to herself, or sometimes isolated herself from everyone.

This was an experience Deremiah had to go through, because even though she was a kind, creative and loving person, his mother couldn't handle pressure. Deremiah says the experience made him much more sensitive about loving people no matter where they are. It caused him to be aware that all people have problems.

In life we prize many things. We prize being popular or being smart, being beautiful or being talented, and all of those things that supposedly make us better than other people. But, there are so many amazing people who are not bright, or who have mental and physical challenges.

There are people who are not beautiful or not talented and yet are so amazing beyond our comprehension, because all people have value.

So many successful people have so many challenges, and we hopefully learn over time to accept people where they are - to understand and value them for the good things we find in their life and help them with the things that are not good.

We've all got those places in our lives, things that we're not good at, and areas that we have serious problems.

In South Chicago, Deremiah was living in a basement, going to a drug and gang infested school where kids were literally being thrown off of third floor balconies. His mom couldn't even give him bus fare, so he had to walk three miles to school.

Deremiah spent almost two months being maneuvered from one desk to the next, because in his English classroom there were no open seats. Every day he would come into the classroom and have to find a desk from somebody who was absent. He couldn't take a seat until after the bell rung and everybody was seated. There were times when kids would come to class late and he would have to get up and go and stand in the back of the class. Even the teacher rebuked him for being in someone's seat.

There were times when Deremiah was homeless and didn't know where he was going to move next, and times when he was put out of relatives' houses because of his mother's mental illness.

By age 16, Deremiah was on the verge of committing suicide. He was that unhappy with his life, and he hated the experience that he was dealing with, but luckily there were people coming into his life who cared.

His English teacher flunked him and he had to re-take the class in the summer. Luckily, this time the new teacher took an interest in Deremiah and his story. She taught him English, but she also loved him and nurtured him.

Deremiah told me, "In an amazing way I can see God showing up in my life and blessing me to have the experience to meet people who really cared about people. When I look back on that experience, that's the real essence of what you're talking about in your book ... about small things making a big difference."

Those were the small things that made a big difference for Deremiah. It was the people who were coming into his life who really cared, and that was the only thing that gave him the courage to continue. That's what really changed his life.

When you look at Deremiah's story, you think it isn't right he should have had to experience this, but he says what he learned was that it was the greatest thing that ever happened to him, because no matter what happens in our economy, and no matter what happens in our culture and our society, because of that experience he knows that it's people that really make the difference. It's people that do the small things that make a huge difference in your life. That gift changed his life forever.

Deremiah pulled himself up with the help of others and then went back to the South Side of Chicago to help teens who were at risk of suicide. He worked in the schools to identify people at risk and made sure they had someone who would listen and care.

And so there came a day when I invited Deremiah to jvAlert Live and he decided to fly to Philadelphia from Chicago to spend the weekend, bringing the special joy that he always brings with him wherever he goes.

One night, we took a walk through the parking lot and sat in my car to talk away from the crowds, and I asked about his life.

Deremiah has so much love for people because he knows some of the people you are talking to today, who are smiling in your face, are wearing a mask. They're really going through a tough time and they don't really know how to be real with people and just let them know .

Deremiah told me ...

"If they only knew that there were people like you and like me, and like some of the other people we know, who would pull them over to the side and take time out with them and talk to them about it - it would be unbelievable. You were the first person, Ken, that ever really did that. We sat in that car and you remember that night. You heard my story and that's when you know you are dealing with quality people, when you've got a man who's running a seminar, who should be focused on what he's got to do tomorrow. It's 10:30, 11 at night and he's listening to your story when he probably should be in bed sleeping to get ready to deal with the two to three hundred people at the seminar the next day, but you took time out to listen to what I had to share.

Not only did you do that, but you turned around and you made a story that was hidden to people revealed. And you didn't do it for riches or wealth or to exploit something for financial gain. You did it because you love people and you know how humane and powerful my story is, and I really honor you and appreciate you for doing that."

As a result of our conversation, I decided to feature Deremiah and his story at the special event I was planning, and to help him with his goal of helping teenagers at risk of suicide.

I'd written my book, *Impact: How to Get Noticed, Motivate Millions and Make a Difference in a Noisy World* and somewhere along the way I developed the somewhat crazy idea that if you are going to teach someone how to do something, you should prove you can do it.

I was teaching people how to get their ideas, products and services out to millions of people and I needed a way to prove I could do it, so I selected a handpicked group of people I called the Impact

Action Team to personally mentor and demonstrate exactly what it takes to do it – by actually doing it.

People who were interested in being on the team filled out a 126 question document which asked them about their passions, skills and goals, and I picked 18 of them to experience the excitement of making a real difference.

Each person had dreams of making a difference with their own set of goals, and through the experience of doing it together and helping Deremiah, they were able to learn the skills that they could apply to their own missions in life.

For my live event – in addition to the Impact Action Team – I invited a world-class group of faculty members to help give instruction in all of the techniques you can use to get ideas, products and services out to millions.

Brendon Burchard came and taught about how to leverage non-profit organizations and their existing communities and resources to reach millions. Frank Sousa talked about using video and distributing it to a huge audience. Warren Whitlock taught the attendees how to use book publishing to gain credibility and visibility; Sanyika Calloway Boyce coached the team in getting on radio and television; Dr. Ron Capps showed us how to use social media; Felicia Slattery gave us tips on public speaking and developing a signature speech; Mary Mazzullo taught the team how to leverage photography, and that's just a few examples of the amazing people who worked with our team.

I also invited people who were interested in learning more about these techniques to come, and we managed to have about 125 people gather in the suburbs of Philadelphia

We divided into small groups, each with a particular focus so we could develop ideas and set goals. There were groups in charge of developing a simple, clear message, website development, video production, social media, speaking, radio and television, book publishing, press and public relations, corporate sponsorships and more.

By the end of the event we had developed a clear message and a clear plan to reach millions, and over the next 30 days we were able to get that message out to 19.1 million people in 30 days.

You can view a short video that tells the story of what came next when I took the Impact Action team and put them on the stage at Brendon Burchard's Life's Golden Ticket Event at:

http://speakupsavelives.org/?p=136

Over the course of a single weekend at Brendon's event, the Impact Action Team was able to develop resources and commitments to get the simple message of hope for people at risk of teen suicide out to an additional 1.9 million people.

Keep reading to discover what Impact Action Team Members Michael Savoie and Cheri Sigmon have to say about how this impacted their lives.

# Chapter 6
## "Because I Miss Dany"

By Impact Action Team member Micheal Savoie,
from the www.SpeakUpSaveLives.org blog

When you grow up with someone, you take them for granted. They are a part of your life, and their part in your life is filled with joys and sorrows as kids tend to go from angelic to mischievous, depending on the weather. My cousin Dany would have been 43 on July 12th.

I spent most of my waking hours with Dany and his older brother Christian exploring, pretending and running from each other. Chris and I used to run away from Dany most of the time, since older kids tend to be cruel to the youngest.

Then we grew up and went our separate ways. I moved from Pennsylvania to Florida, Chris moved to California and Dany moved to Cancun, Mexico. The distance did not help us keep in touch with each other, and having been a loner most of my life, I was not one for initiating conversations, writing letters, etc.

I did hear more from Chris than I did from Dany, and one day, February 1, 2003, I heard from my parents that Dany had taken his own life after he had discovered that he had cancer of the larynx. Shock was not the only thing I felt.

**Guilt.**

I should have been there for him. We all believe that we can make it on our own, and then when someone you know, someone close as a brother, takes their own life, you wonder what effect you could have had.

What impact could I have had?

Beating myself up for the lack of communication, I really sank into a depression. The worst part of the whole situation for me was the fact that I should have maintained contact with Dany.

Why am I dredging up these raw emotions and exposing them for you?

The answer is really only one word:

**LISTEN.**

Hear what your friends and family are saying. You may have some troubled teens in your family. Teens are at a point in their lives where they feel isolated. They want to feel independent, yet they also feel left out from their friends' lives because of cruelty (kids are cruel after all - especially groups) or disagreements.

The reason for their isolation does not matter nearly as much as the fact that it is eating away at their will to live.

Sometimes (I have had this feeling before in a particularly troubling time of isolation from my family and despair at my circumstances) they feel that their life is not worth living, the pain is too unbearable, and that by taking their own life, they would be getting revenge on the people who make them feel so isolated.

"That'll show them!"

Listen to them.

**Then GIVE!**

G - Greet and meet: talk to others, smile, say hello, and ask them how they are doing...

I - Involve yourself: find a cause you can support, volunteer, and pledge resources to

V - Validate others: tell others that they matter - especially family members and friends that you tend to see daily but may take for granted - give genuine compliments

E - Empathize: be a listening ear, take time to be fully present; don't try to solve - just acknowledge someone's feeling or hurt

By following this formula, you are showing teens that you care. Empathy is a catalyst for bonding, and can help you reel in the teen that has started to distance himself or herself from the world around them.

I cannot profess to be an expert, but the people at SpeakUpSaveLives.org like Deremiah Phillips have shown me what taking an extra minute with someone who may just need a smile can do for that person! The goal for our group is to save our teens one at a time. But I have selfishly added my own agenda to this project.

I am doing it because I still miss Dany Savoie!

Micheal Savoie

Micheal Savoie began his writing career as a contributing author for *Amiga World Magazine* when the Commodore Amiga was in the midst of a confusing time in its product cycle. He managed to get two stories into print, and then the Amiga vanished from the face of the earth.

Undaunted, Micheal received a Bachelor's Degree in Business Administration from Saint Leo University, and then his Microsoft Certified Systems Engineer certification and began to work online. After meeting some extremely brilliant marketers at jvAlert Live in

Orlando, Florida in 2007, it became inevitable that Micheal would go all out in his online marketing business.

Micheal helps people who may be struggling to get their business online by blogging about his successes and struggles. He also does a weekly Internet Radio talk show on Tuesdays at 11 AM Eastern called The Blogging With Micheal Show, where he discusses Online Marketing, Social Media and Blogging.

http://bloggingwithmicheal.com

# Chapter 7

## "Creating Advocates"

*How to build raving fans*
*Growing Into Impact*
By Action Team Member Cheri Sigmon

My dad was a life-long entrepreneur. He built his own radio station from the ground up and did that for over 40 years before he retired. He reared our family and took care of us. He made sure to send us to college. It was a lot of fun growing up in that environment. He's probably the reason why I've always had that entrepreneurial bug in the back of my mind.

Because of watching my dad, I don't ever want to give up. I saw not only how successful he was, but also how hard he worked. He had a strong work ethic. He believed in helping others and knew that you reap what you sow. He always shares what he has.

As a small business owner, he helped employ people. I found that inspiring. I believe small business is the life-blood of the American economy.

Dad had the biggest impact on me, not because of what he said, but because of what he did and how he lived. People can say a lot of things about how they are or what they believe, but it's what you do that really makes you who you are. He taught us to treat other people the way you would want to be treated.

The way my dad treated other people in his business taught me a lot. His work ethic, how honest he was, and how much he cared stand out. He had gentleman's agreements, like the old-fashioned days where your word was your bond. Sometimes he lost money doing that, but his word was his bond and he did what he said he would do.

Mostly, it's a lot of little things that left the biggest impression on me. He helped people in the community, went caroling, and made sure we shared from our blessings. He taught us to share and do whatever you can to help others. It's important not to take the blessings we have for granted.

## Under the radar

Around 1994-95, I was online but under the radar. I was on the first ever marketing cruise down to South America along with Ted Nicholas and other big names. I didn't take my charity or business online at that time, but what I did was websites. At the time, I was honing my skills, learning website security. I was opening up a notepad document, coding websites manually, and setting up the security for the sites.

It was more of a hobby than a business. I had a few sites of my own, including a 3-letter domain. I let it go. Someone else has it now. I wish I had held onto it. So if you ever get a three-or 4-letter domain, don't let it go! I learned that one the hard way.

## Stepping Out

The first time I found out about jvAlert and Ken McArthur was online. Somebody sent me a link for jvAlert Live in Orlando. Ronda Del Boccio (co-author of this book) was one of the first people I met. I remember that vividly.

When I read the sales copy for the event, it wasn't really hard sell. It sounded like people were having a good time as well as getting things done, and that was important to me. I decided that if I could make even one good contact or get one good idea at the event, it would be well worth the minimal cost to attend.

I was ready for something new. For me, it was a no-brainer. If I get just one good idea or meet one good friend or business contact, it would be worth the trip. Plus, I was ready for a break. I took the "dive," and I'm glad I did.

jvAlert was much different from the seminars I've been to. So many of them are hard sell or quick-sell, in and out pitch-fests. You go there, have the event, and everybody splits and goes home. Ken's events are different. Come early to have dinner before the event. Meet people while you're there. Stay up all hours of the night talking (on couches!) Then there's the networking breakfast to keep connecting afterward.

The feel is definitely professional but also collegial. It's more friendly and family-like. You sit down, have a conversation and build relationships. That's very unique. After coming to Ken's events, I'm spoiled. Other events work like this: you come, you get pitched, and you leave.

At that event, I made a good personal connection meeting Ronda Del Boccio and Molly Flagtail (Ronda's guide dog). I picked up a package at the event that I wasn't quite ready for, but I keep adding content and getting things in place. When I'm ready to go, the materials will all be there for me to use.

That's another thing I like about the event. There are great resources for the toolkit to choose, along with the great people.

My very first impression of Ken McArthur was that he was different, because he truly cared for people. He wasn't just there to sell stuff. He has a very big heart. And I sensed that he had a strong sense of integrity about him.

79

I believe you should follow your instinct. Like my father, I've made a number of "gentlemen's agreements" over time, and sometimes I have been burned. But with Ken, he has integrity and he will never burn you.

He's one of the good guys in business. Joel Comm called him "The Nicest Guy on the Internet." I think he's one of the nicest guys I've ever met period, online or offline. He exudes friendliness and caring, and he has integrity. That sums up ken McArthur in a nutshell.

I started to do more with my real passion.

## A Passion for Wieners

One of my main passions is dogs. That's why I gravitated to Molly Flagtail. I ran a charity event called the Longest Wiener Dog Contest to find the longest dachshund. It was a fundraiser and awareness-builder for the ASPCA and dachshund rescue.

I wanted to start with a charity to build community around the cause and find out what the community wanted and would buy before writing a book or developing other products. I think that's the correct way. Identify what people want and need, then find something that will fill the desire.

Building the online community, I've collected a list and a community of dog-lovers dedicated to preventing animal cruelty. I've surveyed and grown the relationships. Many of them have sent in success stories of animal rescue and rehabilitation.

Some stories are about an animal that has helped the human who adopted them. Others are where the animal has overcome a challenge of its own. It's all about the animal-human bond. Now I know a book of animal success stories is something people want.

**Stepping Out for Impact**

The Impact Action Team appealed to me because it brought together a community doing something that had never been done before. The goal was to help prevent teen suicide. We started www.SpeakUpSaveLives.org. We reached over 19 million people in 30 days.

People from all walks of life came together, got training and made a huge impact. It had a personal appeal to me because people coming back from the war zone of any era come back and have issues. Not just the returning soldiers, but their teens and other family members, too. And the same principles would help families worldwide, not only teens in the US. It's a good resource.

I worked with Carrie Wilkerson on research. That's one of my skill sets. We all sat around a table in Philadelphia mapping things out and figuring out what skill sets everyone brought to the project. One of the skills I brought to the table that she quickly recognized was research.

I'm able to do research and bring statistics together quickly, and we needed it done at lightning speed. Research is what shapes how the project moves forward.

I joined the Impact Action Team not just for the project, but also because of the concept of learning how to make a bigger impact. Also, the people. I made the commitment not knowing what cause we would focus on, yet I knew it would be a good cause that I would support. I knew I would learn something valuable, and the team would change a lot of lives.

**The Big Top**

We had an opportunity to reach a lot of people at Brendon Burchard's event called Life's Golden Ticket. It was a huge circus event.

The people doing the photography and PR – the things that were up front – stood out for me. I am normally working behind the scenes. Watching the media people be their buoyant, lively selves really caught my interest, because it's such a different side.

After we got to Brendon's big-top event, being present and observing how the whole event came together was amazing for me. We actually went on stage and did the outreach program, which was a big deal for me since I'm mostly behind-the-scenes. There was so much preparation before that big moment.

Being immersed in that circus environment reminded me of being a child at a camp meeting. That's what folks in the south have during the summer. It's a revival. It's a very peaceful feeling to me, because I remember singing songs with my grandparents and other people there. I was thinking about this during the Life's Golden Ticket event.

The type of people Brendon attracted to his event were warm, energetic and receptive. You could feel positive energy flowing inside the tent. It felt like we were making an impact even as we were doing the event, even though we were just kicking off our efforts to stop teen suicide.

**Commitment**

We passed out cards asking everyone how many people they could reach. It was a pledge to take the message to them. Through this group of people, how many people could we reach through leverage? It was a multiplying effect.

We collected that information, so we knew how many could be reached. Some people could only reach a few, but some could reach huge numbers because of their Rolodex or media contacts.

Now that I've been on the Impact Action Team, I've shifted from only being behind-the-scenes research. I'm not as shy about being out front in social media and other public-facing efforts. Now I've done a video, and before I would never have done that. I got over being camera shy. I have a lot of videos on YouTube and Vimeo, plus a Twitter feed for the Longest Wiener Dog competition.

I'm now more out in public. This helped for wiener dog events in the DC area and MeetUp groups (http://www.meetup.com).

MeetUp groups are a great way to get together around a cause. There are groups for dog lovers and for just about anything you can imagine. The connection is first made online to set up the group, but the whole purpose is to meet the "old fashioned way" – offline.

That's how I connected with various dachshund groups. There is even a "DachsFest" (Dachshund festival) for dachshund owners, including wiener dog races and other activities.

**Invest in Your Dream**

I recommend you take some time out of your day to make an investment in yourself and do something different. Reach out and connect with people, online, off-line or both. Whatever your dream is, find people you can relate to. Find people who have common interests.

When you connect with like-minded people, it will energize you to get to wherever you want to go. It will help expand your horizons, develop your skill sets, but most important, it will help you focus on your dream so you can map out a plan and get to that dream.

Open your mind. Open your horizons to create the impact you want to make.

# Chapter 8
## "Passion"

Miro Grudzinski, who attended Brendon Burchard's Life's Golden Ticket event, responded to the Impact Action Team's message of hope.

Miro was born on May 30th, 1956 in Poland into what he calls, "a lower middle-class family." His parents came from generations of farmers, and his father was a low ranking officer in the Polish army. Miro also had two sisters who loved and supported him.

Finances were a challenge, but he was blessed with loving parents and the support of his extended family. His family bonds and social life were very strong and based on the deep faith he carries with him to this day. In the summers, Miro worked on the farms of his relatives and learned early the value of a good day's work.

This experience created a strong platform of support, respect for his elders, and the caring environment they built for him.

Miro says ...

> "I believe all these experiences from the past created, from one side, a strong social bond and a respect to the elders -- to our grandfathers and our parents who are giving us this basic foundation of our relationships and this environment to give us sensitivity and care.
>
> Not only about our self, but about the responsibilities which are slowly coming as we grow, and at the same time giving us an environment of comfort, security and belonging. We were not left as children or as teenagers or boys and girls dealing with our own problems, but being with the cousins

... there was always this joyful experience of team work with the kids, competing and fooling around, and at the same time there was extremely strong development of the maturity, sense of the respect to the work ethic, accountability for the tasks which were given to us".

Miro was experiencing the growing responsibilities and pleasures of becoming a young man. His father allowed him to ride his motorcycle, and then when his father was able to obtain his very first car, he was kind enough to entrust its care to Miro. He even let him drive it.

Miro's father was a photographer. He took many pictures, both in connection with his work in the Army and for postcards he created from his photographs. Miro soon started earning extra money by selling the postcards.

Miro was inspired by his father's kindness, work ethic and service for his country.

Unfortunately, the good times were interrupted tragically when Miro's father passed away in May of 1972 at the age of 46 while on duty at his military base. His death came suddenly. The doctors were unable to determine the reason for his death, but this experience had an unbelievable impact on Miro, his mother, sisters and family.

After three days of crying when he saw his father lying in the coffin, Miro put his hands on his father's chest and made a vow to be the best man and to make him proud that he was his son, and to care about others.

The death left his mother with children to care for, and Miro at 15 years old, became the head of his family.

As the widow of a military officer, Miro's mother was struggling financially and she had difficulty collecting her benefits from the military. Miro experienced firsthand the challenges the widows and orphans of military personnel have to go through.

The hard things that his mother was experiencing inspired Miro to recognize how many widows there are from our uniformed service personnel, our armed services, police, firefighters and so many others who protect us and serve us. There are so many people out there serving us and yet at any time their life could be cut short early, and people are left behind like Miro and his family.

Miro's mother was like a rock. She wasn't bitter. She devoted her strength and everything she had towards her children to make sure that they had everything they needed in life, so they could grow and finish their schooling. Their lives were driven by faith and by their ethics, morals, and beliefs.

Because of those beliefs, Miro's father had refused to sign up for the Socialist party in Poland, which cost him the ability to advance in his career. Miro's roots were very strong, and his beliefs based on the importance of the freedoms that his father treasured so highly.

Poland as a country had always been a nation of open hearts, open minds, and open arms for people who were striving and looking for freedom. Oppressed people had flooded into Poland from around the world as a refuge.

When his father passed away, Miro was in school and times were very harsh. His sister was studying to become a nurse and he was studying electrical engineering. He told his mother that he was going to quit, but his mother told him if he left the school he would have to go on his own. That was a shock for Miro and he decided to stay and finish school.

By the age of 20, Miro graduated and started on his electrical engineering career working for the government. But he quickly discovered a desire to make money, to make progress in his life and find some independence.

Miro started working on the side in the export business and soon was doing very well, but he had an urge to go back to school. He chose to study economics and management of tourism and recreation. While continuing to educate himself, Miro worked as a paramedic where he learned about trauma situations. He admired the tremendous dedication of the nurses, ambulance workers, firefighters and police (despite hard work and low pay) and the value that they bring to society.

Miro met his future wife at the university while working 48 hours a week as a paramedic working two 24 hour shifts and using the other five days to attend classes. In his third year at the university, they got married and then graduated together with a Master's degree.

Poland was under martial law and the Solidarity Movement was underway, pushing Poland towards democracy. There was no possibility for leisure time in the political environment for Poland. The borders were closed and there was no tourism, so in 1984 when Miro received an opportunity to go abroad to work in the field of electrical engineering, he took the job working on nuclear power plants in Czechoslovakia.

It was a lonely life, because his wife was still in Poland living with her parents. He was only able to come back on occasional weekends. He was working, saving his money and working on the side in his business again, making progress. In 1986 he finally finished the job, returning financially secure.

Miro took a management job for a non-profit organization. He gained the experience of working with an organization with thousands and thousands of members and also working with many corporations. Like his father before him, Miro encountered a politically charged environment and was being pressured to join the political party to advance.

With his advancement limited, Miro opened his own company in 1987 using the connections he had made to act as a broker and deal maker between various customers and suppliers in several countries. The finances were going well.

Miro had been asking his wife to move to Canada, and in 1989 he and his wife immigrated. They started a business in Brampton, Ontario.

Following his passion, Miro began work on a project that had been near and dear to his heart for a long time.

In 1995, Miro and his wife became Canadian citizens, which was a fulfillment of his childhood vision and dream as a nine year old boy, when in 1965 he saw a Canadian flag for the first time during an international fair in Poznan, Poland. A deep desire to visit and complete his destiny in Canada was implanted in his heart.

Miro was involved in the community work and established and registered a foundation for families and children with special needs called "Hope for the Future".

In July 2002, with a group of strong supporters, he started his stewardship mission and organized the first annual "Hope for the Future" Family Picnic. Notable people in attendance were the Mayor, federal and municipal politicians, and the famous Canadian icon, artist Charles Pachter.

Loyal to his citizenship and civic commitments, Miro also dedicated countless hours during elections to support federal, provincial and municipal politicians regardless of their political affiliation. He always took a stand to support those whose major mandate is the welfare of the needy and less fortunate.

When terrorists attacked the United States on September 11th, 2001, many Canadians were moved by the tragedies, and a large group of Canadians were part of the workers that streamed into New York City to help rescuers after the fall of the World Trade Center Towers. That event left Miro changed forever.

Miro had met Charles Pachter and seen his art in January 2002, but now he was inspired by his famous painting "Side, by Side - The Painted Flags," which was dedicated to Ralph Gerhardt of Toronto and all victims of the 9/11 disaster. Miro started his new life journey to promote the spirit of unity, brotherhood, friendship and solidarity between Canada and the United States of America, and to honor all uniformed public servants.

Using art in different media as the most powerful expression of the human spirit, and engaging art to create financial resources to support those in need, are the primary goals of the devoted professionals who have joined in this great and fascinating life voyage.

Miro's "Side By Side We Are One" is a nonprofit foundation specializing in raising money and providing programs for 9/11 victims and service personnel on a global basis.

It raises critical support funds and awareness organically, and in conjunction with global not-for-profit (NFP) foundations supporting similar causes.

I first met Miro coming off the stage after speaking at Brendon Burchard's "Life's Golden Ticket Event" with the Impact Action Team.

Stacks of boxes of blindingly bright T-Shirts were all around him announcing "Side By Side We Are One", and before I could turn around Miro had me in one, excitedly snapping my picture.

Miro was on a mission.

His passion was to promote the spirit of unity, brotherhood, friendship and solidarity between Canada and the United States of America, and to honor all uniformed public servants.

And he was very intense.

Literally, Miro wanted to change the world. How he was going to do that, I wasn't sure, but it wouldn't be for lack of passion.

Miro decided that he should go to my jvAlert Live event in Las Vegas despite the fact that he really didn't have funds to do it. He seemed to think that the funds would magically appear.

Who knows how he did it, but when jvAlert Live started, Miro was there. He was staying over a half hour away from the event location to save money, but he was buying everything in sight with a borrowed credit card.

Every speaker's program was exactly what he needed for his grand vision.

Finally, I had to talk to him and tell him that he really shouldn't be buying all of these packages.

Miro argued passionately with me that I didn't understand and pleaded with me to meet him very early the next day so he could talk to me and show me his plan.

I wasn't the only person who was concerned about Miro. His passion was making some of the attendees cringe a bit. Ever meet someone with too much passion about something?

Early, early the next morning I met with Miro and discovered that he slept overnight outdoors so he could meet with me.

Miro pulled out a stack of papers and pictures.

He had a massive plan, business structure and pictures of hundreds of officials and people he had met who were involved in his project, including the Prime Minister of Canada and members of Parliament.

And then he told me that he would have his own trailer by the time we met next.

That was hard to believe.

He was standing there with no money in his pockets and thousands of miles just to get back home.

And he did it …

At the next jvAlert Live, he was there with his brand new truck and trailer.

Since I met him, Miro has been tireless in supporting our uniformed service personnel and the relationships between countries and peoples.

To help commemorate the united efforts during the 9/11 crisis, Miro traveled back to where it all started to participate in a number of activities in New York City.

Miro's story was just beginning. Through his attendance at jvAlert Live events his knowledge and mission grew, but his primary focus was still to promote bilateral relationships between Canada and the United States of America and to assist in the wellness, rehabilitation, physical, emotional and mental care and support for the uniformed public servants and their families.

Miro wanted to enrich our relationships, heritage and fruitful cooperation through his projects, programs, events, functions and rallies, and to support projects and programs which benefit the disabled officers and soldiers, veterans and men and women in uniform.

He committed to provide assistance for widows and orphans left behind by the brave men and women who died heroically while on duty serving, providing and protecting our citizens, communities and our countries, as well as citizens and their families, who have suffered acts of terror and violence.

That impact is immeasurable, but is passion enough? We need more than passion to pull us through hard times.

On Friday, January 27th, 2012, Miro took his own life in his home.

Miro was a friend and tireless supporter and member of the Impact and jvAlert Live Family who served his adopted country faithfully and uniformed service personnel around the world with a passion impossible to replace.

The Impact Factor: How Small Actions Change the World

# Chapter 9

## "Is Your Best Stuff Still On the Drawing Board?"

Friday, June 3rd in Denver, Colorado, jvAlert Live expert Rick Butts is being held down on a bed on the third floor of the Denver Health Care Hospital and the room is filled with nearly every nurse, resident, orderly and employee on the floor.

Rick is drenched in his own blood, and so are they.

The surgeon, who had performed a cancer removal surgery on Rick earlier that morning, was on top of him trying to stop the artery in his neck from bleeding.

How quickly life changes!

Only a few short months ago, Rick had been healthy and on the expert panel at jvAlert Live in Denver, and now he was fighting for his life.

Rick had spent a long journey to get to that place. In his own words:

> "In the process of raising myself up from a booze and dope head musician I devoured all the self-help, success, and motivation literature I could find. I parlayed that knowledge and life experience into a career as a motivational speaker, traveling internationally to give my keynote speech at conventions."

Rick was blazingly successful as a keynote speaker. If you had a chance to hear him, it was magic. But life turns on a dime, and now Rick is fighting for his. Luckily the room full of medical experts managed to get the bleeding stopped, but that is just the start of a long battle, and it got Rick to thinking …

"While I was in danger, I made no deals with God. I was ready to go – and the life I had was frankly not bringing me much happiness. On reflection, I wondered why I was so apathetic about the outcome, and now I believe I know why.

I have simply not been doing the kind of work I was capable of, and letting illness and momentum keep me on the sidelines."

Now Rick is realizing that for him …

The best stuff is still on the drawing board

Is your life still on the drawing board?

You have no idea when your health may change your outlook on life completely.

If your life is on the drawing board, you need to get started today, because things don't always happen in your favor.

The responding nurse could have been a minute too late for Rick and in an instant he could have been gone … with magic still left on the drawing board.

Don't let it happen to you.

There is the story of a preacher who got up one Sunday and announced to his congregation: "I have good news and bad news. The good news is, we have enough money to pay for our new building program. The bad news is, it's still out there in your pockets."

So what do you have in your pockets today?

# Chapter 10
## "Taking Action"

If you are passionate or desperate, you take action.

If you don't take action, you aren't feeling the passion or desperation enough.

If you are truly hungry, then you will find a way to eat and nothing will stop you.

If you are truly passionate, then you will find a way and nothing will stop you, until you die or the passion or desperation goes away.

Death stops all of us — for this world anyway — so let's talk about what we do when we are passionate or desperate enough to take action.

Lately I've been talking to people who have a lot of passion and/or a lot of desperation.

Those people have two choices:

1.  They can do more of what they are doing now.
2.  They can do new things.

When you are desperate, you try new things.

If what you are doing right now isn't working, the tendency is to try something else.

Desperate people typically try a lot of new things -- and most end in failure.

The most common reason why is NOT because there aren't good things to do.

It's because desperate people don't make the in-depth effort to make something succeed.

In fact, they may not have the time or resources to make the in-depth commitment they must make in order to succeed.

> For want of a nail the shoe was lost.
> For want of a shoe the horse was lost.
> For want of a horse the rider was lost.
> For want of a rider the battle was lost.
> For want of a battle the kingdom was lost.
> And all for the want of a horseshoe nail.

When you are passionate, you tend to do the same things.

I know thousands of people personally who think that they have "the" answer for making the world a better place.

They are focused, and some of them are unbelievably passionate about it!

In fact, some of them are so focused that they say and do the same things over and over expecting success to happen from their powerful persistence.

Persistence is a powerful thing.

I've seen passionate people do amazing things, just from one thing that they keep beating over people's heads until they have to listen.

And I've seen people take foolish risks with their time and possessions to pursue dreams that only bring them heartache.

Action, passion and persistence, even combined with desperation, are not enough to guarantee success.

Sorry. Even if you combine it with brilliance, luck and truly deliver massive value, there is no guarantee.

If you have success, there is no guarantee you will keep it.

So what's your choice?

- You can give up.
- You can keep taking actions to move you towards your goals.
- Or … you can go deep.

Depth of action is what makes you more likely to succeed.

If you give up with little effort, you will likely fail.

So many times I see people trying something for a week or two and saying, "That doesn't work!"

In many cases what they are doing will work if they keep at it and go in-depth.

So how do you go in-depth when you are desperate?

Focus.

Start with the very core for small success and build out from there.

You need audience, a product or service, and conversion, so start with the simplest actions that will get you some of all three.

Then go in-depth.

Go from "Simple" to "Deep." All you need is a small success to make you see that you can build forever.

Everyone knows you need to set goals.

What's not as well known is that there are lots of mistakes you can make in the process.

Here are 13 of the Worst Mistakes you can make when setting your goals:

- Setting too many goals
- Not being specific
- Creating goals that can't be measured
- Setting goals that aren't relevant
- Developing goals that aren't realistic
- Setting goals that have no time limit.
- Not putting goals in writing.
- Setting goals that are too easy.
- Framing goals negatively.
- Not understanding why you want to achieve a goal.
- Not setting priorities for your goals.
- Setting goals for things that you can't control.
- Setting goals that you don't want to achieve.

If you want to be successful in reaching your goals, you need to do two things well:

1. Start
2. Finish

Everything in between is just filler!

# Chapter 11
## "Measured Results"

The impact each of us has on the lives of others can definitely seem random. The reason is because all those chance encounters, minor moments and unexpected turns of events might seem to be beyond anyone's control.

Let's begin with two baseline understandings before diving into the concept of tracking and measuring results.

The first baseline understanding is that everyone will have unplanned and unintended impact on other people and the world, for good and for ill. Probably there will be some of both in everyone's life.

The second baseline understanding is that the apparently most insignificant moments can be the most powerful touchstones of impact. The well-timed smile, kind word or insight can change the course of someone's life.

Stopping there would leave impact entirely up to chance or divine planning or things beyond anyone's conscious control. There is so much more to creating an impact, and that is where measuring results comes into play.

Why measure?

Take a moment to imagine the power that tracking and measuring can bring to having an impact. Let's start with something anyone can understand, whether or not you have done it yourself: weight loss.

Changing weight is all about measuring. You can measure things like calories in, calories burned, minutes of exercise, carbs, protein, fruits and vegetables…and the list of things that might be calculated, counted and catalogued in order to lose weight goes on and on.

Measuring over time paints a picture of your impact on your weight. Patterns emerge over time. Perhaps a certain food slows your weight loss or maybe exercising at a certain time of day helps you feel more energized. You may notice you need to avoid certain people, restaurants or temptations in order to stay on track. One food plan may not work for you at all. Eating five small meals a day might be worse for you than eating three meals.

Setting a goal or intention is NOT what provides the power to cause the desired outcome. The Franklin Covey research firm polled 15,000 people regarding their resolutions. A full third of the respondents broke their promises before the end of January. Other surveys show that 92 per cent of Americans who make resolutions drop them by the end of January.

That means neither intention nor setting a goal to have an impact are effective means of producing the desired outcome. Leaving impact up to chance is just as unsatisfying and unproductive. Measuring results is what provides the tools to fuel change.

Looking at results over time is just the beginning of measuring impact. Deeper analysis is necessary to know how to interpret and track which actions brought about what results. Measuring results and tracking the trends over time bestow the ability to increase what is working and diminish what is not working.

# Chapter 12

## "Creative Ideas"

Creative ideas change the world, so go out and make something happen.

Although it wasn't at the same time and surely not the same YMCA, Hugh MacLeod and I have this in common: we both had the experience of being young, living creatively, struggling and chasing our creative dreams while living in a YMCA.

My YMCA was in Pasadena and I got there from Florida in a VW bug with no spare tire.

I'd been singing and playing my original music in small clubs in the Tampa Bay area in Florida, and it was time to head for the "Big Time."

I was feeling the pain of breakup, the fear of the future and the aching stench of failure hanging in the humid air of Florida. There seemed to be no alternative in the immediate future that included staying where I was.

I needed to get creative, because sometimes we need to create a whole new life if we really don't like the current one.

It seems as though life revolves around "Turning Points," and this was a time for life to move in an entirely different direction.

Which brought me to the not so creative thought, "What better place to be creative than California?"

Creative people often come to L.A. to find their creative dreams. Whatever you do for a living, it seems like everyone there is chasing a bigger dream, and so one day I decided just to go there.

The timing was good because I was going nowhere fast in Tampa. The finances were not quite so good.

I had a Martin D-35 12 string guitar, a book called, "Los Angeles on 5 Dollars a Day," a VW bug with no spare tire and some gas money with about $20 to spare for expenses.

My "creative" idea was to head for Houston, a city in the middle of "boom times," locate a job that would pay me at least minimum wage so I could earn enough money to make the rest of the trip.

Jumping in the V.W., I drove straight through without stopping to sleep, for over 15 hours, up the peninsula of Florida, across the panhandle, cutting across the southern edges of Alabama, Mississippi and Louisiana and finally arrived at Houston as the sun set in the West.

Unfortunately, there was "no room in the inn."

It was "boom times" in Houston and every cheap motel I passed had a "No Vacancy" sign flashing away, so I took a breath and decided to keep driving. If you want to get where you are going, you have to be persistent.

Realize it's almost as far across Texas as it is cutting through Florida, Alabama, Mississippi and Louisiana, so it took me another almost 12 hours to drive across Texas and find myself on the outskirts of El Paso, which is where for the first time, I blew a tire.

Blowing a tire without any spare would have been a bit more problematic if it had occurred in the early hours of the morning in the vast stretches of Texas – where it seemed there were no people for countless miles and only the company of occasional tumbleweeds. I was blessed.

After driving down the highway on the rim of my tire for five or ten miles, I found a tire store, pulled into the parking lot and waited for the store to open and the sun to rise.

Eventually, the sun did rise and the store did open. Unfortunately, they didn't have a tire that would fit my V.W. bug. So I piled back into my V.W. and with a few directions from the store clerk, headed on the rim of the tire for a junk lot, where I was told I might find a used tire.

This time, I was lucky enough to find two beat-up, used tires for $5 each.

I was good. Not only did I have a tire to drive on, but I also had a spare tire in case something happened.

So $10 poorer, but 2 tires richer, I was back on the road.

I drove through the southern desert, across New Mexico and Arizona, until I reached the state line of California – which is where my replacement tire blew out.

But, I was okay! This time I had a spare tire!

So I changed my tire and pulled out my trusty book, "Los Angeles on 5 Dollars a Day," and found a couple $5 a night motels – dream on about finding $5 a night motels now – chose one in Pasadena and headed that way.

I didn't know anyone, didn't have a job and didn't have a place to stay. My gas money was running out and I only had about $10 left for lodging.

As I got closer, I started hearing a slight flapping noise which got louder and louder as I approached the Pasadena city limits. The tread had started to separate on the replacement tire, so I pulled into the home of the Rose Bowl with the sound of "flap, flap, flap, flap" ringing in my ears.

By the time I reached the motel, it was Saturday night and I knew that I'd have to wait until Monday morning for the employment office to open. That meant two nights at $5 a night and zero reserves, so early on Monday morning I was waiting at the employment office when they opened for the day.

"What kind of job are you looking for?"

"Anything!"

The helpful employment counselor located a job working for an auto paint store. The job was delivering paint to auto body shops in the area and I went to apply.

As only happens in Los Angeles, the manager of the store was a struggling film director who was only managing a paint store to earn a living while he made it big in the film industry. When he heard my story about driving across the country to find fame and glory, he hired me and I started working immediately.

At the end of the day, I had a problem.

There was no money left and no place to stay, so I asked the manager if he would be willing to give me an advance on my paycheck, which wasn't due for at least a week. It was enough for one night's stay in the Pasadena YMCA.

It took me three weeks of paying the daily rate for the YMCA room I found before I could get together enough money together to pay by the week – which was a cheaper rate.

I took a second job working in the evenings in a gas station.

Lots of faith involved in making a move like that, but persistence wins out because countless opportunities are available to anyone.

By the end of three months I found mine when I was offered the editorship of "Recording Engineer/Producer" Magazine, the leading publication for the recording industry in the world.

When you have nothing, create something.

Hugh MacLeod was getting creative too.

Hugh was a struggling copywriter, living in the local YMCA in New York City when he started to doodle on the backs of business cards just to have something to do while he was sitting at a bar.

Hugh landed at the YMCA in Manhattan with only two suitcases and a couple cardboard boxes of belongings, but he had the advantage of a ten-day freelance copywriting job at a Midtown advertising agency.

The next couple weeks were taken up with work, walking around the city and local bars and coffee shops, while being hit five times a day by a strange urge to laugh, sing and cry – all at the same time.

Luckily, the freelance job turned into a full time one.

For Hugh, the little drawings on the backs of business cards were an effort to capture "the intensity, the fleeting nature and the everlasting song of New York City." He had a real job, so he could do what he wanted. There was no need to make money out of his idea and no need to worry about what anyone thought about his drawings.

Hugh is a pretty creative guy. B.L. Ochman called him, "the poster child for unemployed creative types seeking blog fame and fortune."

Those cartoons on the back of business cards eventually lead to Hugh's Blog – Gaping Void – which became the fourth most popular blog in Europe, second most popular in the UK and number 139 worldwide with close to a million page views a month.

Just to give you an idea of his creativity, here's Hugh's description of himself:

"I work as a jester of pharmacology, avoiding lawyers and prolonging the inevitable. I like long walks in outer space. I have already contributed to our gene pool. IP addresses excite me. CSS is often very fun. When cornered I can cook. Folding laundry is a pleasure. Vacuums are useful tools. I am happy to find a decahedron that suits my needs. I am fluent in several forms of gibberish. My loudness scale : DM<ETEK<KP2. I have driven many hybrid cars. I have built stuff. I am intimate with the Maverick Meerkat. I have been audited. I have been to court. I have been to city hall. I have tried love. I vote early and often. I buy art. I incubate things. I have had surgery. I take medicine. I wear glasses often. I never lift my mask. I see dead people and they are dead. I have something no one else can get".

In his book "Ignore Everyone: And 39 Other Keys to Creativity," Hugh talks about how, "The more original your idea is, the less good advice other people will be able to give you".

When Hugh started doing his cartoons on the back of business cards, people thought he was crazy. They encouraged him to find more traditional outlets for his artistic efforts. Why not do cute little greeting cards? It would be easier for the market to digest.

As Hugh says, "You don't know if your idea is any good the moment it's created. Neither does anyone else."

Great ideas shift the power balance, and that almost always means they will be resisted.

When I headed for California in my V.W. bug, there was some resistance to the idea from people I knew. After all, I had no job, no money, I didn't know anyone there and Los Angeles was thousands of miles away from friends and family

I didn't really know what waited for me there or whether it was a good idea. I just knew that I needed to create a new life.

If you need to create something new or you need to change your life in any way, right now is the first opportunity you have to do it.

Success isn't certain. I failed along the way, but failure is a temporary situation on your road to more adventures and opportunities than you can ever imagine – if you keep at it.

If you want to create great ideas, you have to put in the work. Hugh's cartoons on the back of business cards is a very simple idea and he gets asked whether he's worried that someone will rip it off. After all, anyone can doodle on the back of a business card. Hugh says, "Only if they can draw more of them than me, better than me." Hugh puts in the work.

You want to be creative, so make something. Then do it again and again.

Frank Sousa made something. Here is what he says about creating a great idea on the back of a napkin:

> "When I flew across the country for that first jvAlert, I had no idea that I would become as close a friend as I have been to Ken McArthur. It's VERY rare that men get to enjoy the type of closeness and love that we share, and that means a lot to me.

Then at another jvAlert event, I met Mike Koenigs. Mike and I were talking over dinner that night, and he was telling me all the great things he was doing with online video, but it took too long to submit them to all the various video sites. So I suggested we do it from a server in the back end.... Six weeks later I'd built a prototype of Traffic Geyser, and of course Traffic Geyser has become a huge multi-million dollar business... and we designed it on the back of a napkin at jvAlert.

Then of course I sold my interest to Mike and Rocket, (my partners), for an undisclosed 7 figure deal.... which gave me the time and freedom to create my next software product that will be released very soon, Easy Money Bots. Stand by.... And all because of Ken McArthur's request to see if anyone wanted to get together and network.... and of course the famous "Three Guys on a Couch" story that Ken likes to tell".

# Chapter 13

## "Finding Your Audience"

*Your Audience Is Out There Somewhere!*

It doesn't matter who you are, what your opinions might be or even whether you have anything to say worth listening to. Someone is willing to listen to YOU right now.

In fact, they are listening to someone right now and they might as well be listening to you!

But, most likely they aren't.

Even if you have thousands of fans, clients, customers and supporters for your ideas, products and services, you haven't even touched the surface of the audience available to you right now.

As I write this, there are 310,574,391 people in the United States alone and the world has a few more … 6,877,731,978 at last count.

I'm pretty sure you aren't reaching them all.

But, I'm also just as sure that there are THOUSANDS of people who agree with what you want to say — no matter what you think.

### 1. "Who is your Target Audience?"

- What type of audience do you want?
- Are you looking for a particular age, gender, location etc – or stage of life, political interests?
- What are the personality traits, emotions, needs, passions and frustrations of your audience?
- What value or benefit can you bring to the table?
- Who is your ideal customer?

- What kinds of groups or associations would they join?
- What do they dislike?

Try imagining a prototype person who is your main audience.

- Name the person.
- Give them an age.
- An outlook on life.
- A job.
- A family.
- A city to live in.
- Interests.
- An Education.

Do you have more than one audience? Why not list them all out?

- What is cool to these people?
- What impresses them?
- How do they interact?
- Are they technical?
- Are they sophisticated?
- Are they conservative?
- Are they radical

What is the tone of their language?

- Do they use slang?
- Do they want "Just the facts?"
- Are they emotional?
- Are they angry?
- Do they have a history together?

What do they want and need?

- What are they missing?
- What are their problems?
- What do they value?
- What is most important to them?
- What are they least likely to care about?

The best way to spread your message is to start by observing what is already being shared, discussed and admired by your audience.

## 2. "Identify where your audience is and what they do"

- Where do they hang out?
- What activities are they taking part in?
- Are they readers?
- Social animals?
- Do they have their own jargon or lingo?

Talk to your audience

- Do surveys.
- Ask your friends and relatives what things they would look for if they were your potential customers.
- Find online forums that appeal to your audience.
- Research what your competitors are doing.
- Keep on top of what your industry buzz is about for successful target marketing.
- Subscribe to relevant newsletters and publications.
- Use market research to find vendors and content providers.
- Search Google for blogs, profiles and groups.

Look for "Hot Spots"

Where does my target go to …

- Network
- Research
- Read the news
- Catch up with friends
- Be entertained

See who's getting results. Which items are …

- Getting the most buzz
- Gathering responses
- Causing controversy
- Being the most useful

Check your competitors …

Be sure to locate your competitor's online presence to make sure you're heading in the right direction.

- Focus on high-traffic sites, events and profiles …
- Find potential partners, what websites they are on.
- Don't stop researching your target audience.
  Your marketing strategy must keep pace with change.

Check your own analytics…

Google Analytics is a great way to see who refers readers to your site. Check out where your audience comes from and visit those sites. Then check and see where they are going when they leave your site.

### 3. "Find the key influencers"

Who are the key …

- Bloggers
- Marketers
- Experts
- Print Publications
- Media Outlets
- Mavens
- Reporters
- Social Media Addicts

Then figure out what motivates them to move your message out to the masses.

### 4." Engage with Empathy"

You don't stand out in a crowd by standing there and yelling. Think about the boy who cried "Wolf." It works the first time, but after a while people tune you out.

Introduce content or conversations your audience is interested in using a voice that commands respect or affection or they won't listen to you.

Ask …

- What is my audience interested in?
- What would they want to read?
- What do they search for?
- How can I entertain?"

Definitely …

- Be personal
- Be helpful
- Be enjoyable
- Ask questions
- Be human
- Be nice
- Be interesting
- Use their language and jargon
- Share media (pictures, videos, reports) they will connect with

## 5. "Expand the edges"

Reach out to your audience and become part of communities.

- Subscribe to blogs
- Join networks
- Join groups
- Write articles
- Publish a book
- Attend live events
- Speak
- Create useful content
- Comment on blogs and forums
- Set up Google Alerts to track mentions.
- Use StumbleUpon – to discover and read new content
- Introduce yourself – Sending someone a personalized email shows them that you have noticed them and you care about them enough to personally contact them.
- Respond to posts
- Answer questions
- Solve problems

- Make them notice your presence.
- Share interesting content.
- Check out advertisements
- Use Google Trends and Trendrr to search for what is trending now.
- Use Quantcast to get data (size, age, income, education, etc) on your audience.
- Use Technorati to search for hot blogs and posts.
- Use Dan Zarrella's ReTweetability Index and Wefollow.com to find the most influential Twitter accounts by keyword and number of re-tweets.
- Use local geo-targeted directories such as Placeblogger
- Search Facebook fan pages

Find out who and what is popular

- What posts are drawing comments
- What is being retweeted
- What Fan pages have high followers
- What topics are hot today
- What is the news media covering right now
- Which headlines are drawing you in
- What videos are getting the most views

## 6. "Deliver quality solutions"

Think about who you are, what you stand for, and what valuable contributions you can make to your audience.

Be as specific as possible.

- What do you have to say that will surprise your audience?

- What do you want your audience to think, learn, or assume about?
- What impression do you want to convey to your audience?

Solve real problems!

Develop content and delivery platforms (blogs, social network profiles, article sites, forums, etc.) so you have a platform you can communicate your expertise on a consistent basis.

## 7. "Determine your keywords and key phrases"

Develop a list of keywords and key phrases your audience is searching for.

For detailed help on keyword research, view the free video tutorials at http://newbiequickstart.com

Keyword research is a tactic marketers use to help increase search engine optimization (SEO) for bloggers and websites to improve their visibility in search engines.

After you have your keywords, here are a few ways to use them:

- Use Twitter Advanced Search to search on your keywords and phrases and follow interesting people in the results.
- Subscribe to the RSS feed of the results.
- Identify hashtags (these are keywords prefaced with a #) used in posts related to your terms.
- Write tweets using your keywords as hashtags.
- Use Twellow.com to search Business Categories.
- Use Blastfollow.com to follow Twitter users in mass based on subject.

## 8. "Outsource your marketing to find your target audience."

It's easier than ever to find qualified and knowledgeable experts for reasonable rates to create marketing strategies for your company's target audience.

Free resources for list building and outsourcing are available here:

http://budurl.com/123Easy

## 9. "Advertise!"

Who says you have to jump through hoops to build an audience?

It is nice to know that there are targeted, reliable, effective options in paid media to reach consumers in their media of choice.

## 10." Do good!"

All of the above methods really come down to one basic principle. Do good things and you will have all the audience you ever need.

A contest set Kristi Sayles on her path:

> "I entered and won a contest that Mark Joyner was having. That opened doors for me to meet some of the top marketers in the world and even to be interviewed by them. As much as I enjoyed being interviewed, I thought it would be much more fun to be the interviewer, so I bought TalkwithExperts.com and started inviting well known marketers to join me for recorded discussions.
>
> I interviewed the cream of the crop! That led to my being invited to be the host of Mentored by Millionaires - a World Talk Radio Show. I was blessed enough to interview almost all of my favorite marketers: Alan Bechtold, Mark Joyner,

Stephanie J. Hale, Brian Klemmer, Brian Bagnall, Joshua Shafran, Court Cunningham, Matt Bacak, Rob Toth, Scott Lovingood, and one of my ultimate favorites...Ken McArthur!

I'm blessed".

Dr. Mani came to the Internet from India and found a whole new world open to him.

"I first got 'online' when the Internet came to India in late 1995. Yes, that was fifteen years back. My initial excitement came from the thought of having the "world at my fingertips". That hitherto unavailable facility to connect with a human being somewhere else in the world, instantly, easily, and inexpensively, is what got me exploring so many facets of the World Wide Web.

One thing led to another. I discovered my 'hidden' flair for writing. Found people who could help me nurture it, grow it, and then profit from it. Linked that income stream to a non-profit venture I had been thinking about - and which has grown to become the Dr.Mani Children Heart Foundation, raising over $130,000 for charity and sponsoring life-saving heart surgery for 72 children until 2010.

But back then, it was relatively harder to connect with people. True, there were niche online communities... but you had to go out there hunting to find them. And once on them, there were precious few people willing to interact with you. The HUGE lists like i-Sales had a few thousand subscribers. Big forums were populated with hundreds of members at its busiest times. And there were no Facebooks, no MySpaces... no Tobri.coms!

At its core, every online interaction is one between two (or more) PEOPLE, sitting in front of their computer - or more recently, their mobile computing device. And at the core of our existence is our ability to communicate with, relate to, and cherish the "community" of which we are a part. Previously, from necessity, that community had to be local (unless you were a globe-trotter). Today, that community can be ANYWHERE in the world - because places like Tobri.com help connect us, regardless of where we are.

To someone like me who enjoys inter-personal networking, this kind of human-powered community is a gift. Even though I'm an introverted, shy and busy person who may never have had the chance to engage in it to this extent in my offline world alone. And the leverage such a vast network has given to the non-profit work I'm engaged in would surely have not been possible otherwise.

And so I am deeply appreciative of the efforts of Ken McArthur and Chris Moos in creating such a platform, making it a vibrant and colorful network, and growing it into an interactive community - one where I'm happy to devote a (small) part of my busy life, because it fulfills the essential desire we all have as people... The desire to connect and communicate with others like ourselves! Happy New Year 2011 –

Let's meet more often on Tobri :-)"

# Chapter 14

## "Your Social Network"

Joelle Kosmin shared how connecting with people got her through an extremely difficult time in her life.

"I got married in 1989. We had a beautiful life on many levels and I thought we'd be together forever. I thought I'd found the last of the good ones. And for years things were really great.

But something went wrong. There are lots of gory and awful details but I try not to focus on them. Suffice it to say, the man I divorced was far from the man I married. It has been 7 years and it's still the most painful thing that has ever happened to me. But, also the best.

So I began my journey. What I believe to be my real life journey, the gift I was given by the break-up of my marriage. I began to focus on enjoying both my time with my children and my time without.

Through my business networking, I found a free group that worked with the Law of Attraction and the book, *Think and Grow Rich*. That blessing turned into a deeper delving into positivity and internal peace.

At one networking event, I met someone who told me about Internet Marketing and got me to a jvAlert. Lucky me! What an amazing experience and group of people. I hold a special place in my heart for many of the people I met there.

I see all good things in the future".

# Chapter 15

## "You have to Like People!"

By Jane Mark and Phil Basten

Jane: I've wanted to create an impact on people since I was three and learned to talk. My whole life has been creating some sort of impact or another. I always wanted to sing and perform...I still do, by the way. So at the age of three, I was doing whatever I could to sing, to dance, and to do whatever kind of performance I could.

This carried forward in my life. It has always been important to me to do some sort of what I'll label performance. Later in my life when I went into businesses, I still find that desire to perform. And every area of a business has a performance aspect.

I think the desire to make an impact starts very early in a lot of people.

Phil: My desire to make an impact also started early on in my life. When I was in my first school, I realized that complete strangers would have absolutely no trouble coming up and telling me their entire life story.

I would sit there and listen. Even though at that age I didn't give any advice, it was interesting to note that they would reveal to me that much about themselves. They felt they could trust me even though they had never met me before. That was the sort of impact that I've looked for over the years. It wasn't by design, but nevertheless it was there when I made a difference in someone's life

Phil: I was a skinny little wiry thing when I was in early school days. I made friends with this little guy who was a lot smaller than me and a lot smaller than most of the kids. He was nice. We had fun together. I would go to his house sometimes and I knew his parents.

One day I came out of class and noticed the local school bullies were punching him. I saw absolute red. I flew into the middle of them and flattened the two biggest ones. They didn't even know where it came from. I knew at that point that he was a little kid and there was no way in the world I was going to walk away from that.

This little kid needed my help, and he got it. I've followed that theme throughout my life. This bugs Jane sometimes, because I'll get on the phone with someone and they'll start telling me their life story. They'll start telling me all of the problems they have getting started in online advertising.

She gets really mad at me when I start giving out free advice over the phone. I just sit down and talk. I just love sitting down and talking to people and getting to know them.

Jane: He can go on forever. It's a wonderful attribute to have. Being able to teach people what you know. It's the most rewarding part. Forget the money involved in business or anything else. Phil and I both feel strongly about this, because I do a lot of teaching of how our sites work. People love it, because without that, people don't know where to start.

Phil: Jane's the best about describing how things work on the internet. I tend to focus on how people work, because if you don't get to the point of believing you can do this, then you're never going to do it, regardless of how good the tools are.

Jane: It's a good pairing. We work well together. We both love people and love teaching.

My story of making a big impact comes from when I had to go down to Mississippi about ten years ago. It was a memorial service on the anniversary of the murders of Andrew Goodman and Michael Schwerner and James Chaney. Andy was my cousin, and I had to go speak in front of a memorial church service, which is not my thing. My aunt was very old, and so I had to go down.

They didn't tell me this, but I had to give a speech after Jesse Jackson spoke. I don't know if you can imagine the feeling of what it would be to have to give a speech after one of the best orators in the country. I knew he would be a tough act to follow!

I was shaking in my boots at the time, and then I decided if you can follow Jesse Jackson, you can do anything. It's interesting, because Ken is always talking about how you don't always know the ways you impact people. I had no idea I would have this kind of impact on a group of people. It was amazing.

What was very interesting is that because I was Andy's cousin, it almost didn't matter what I said. I connected with these people instantly. Even in the church, these people gave me a rousing round of applause.

When you have someone who was murdered, you don't really want to go down to the state where they were killed, so it took me a lot of courage to go down there without being angry, but I did. I touched those people, and they also touched me.

You don't always know when you're going to have an impact on people or what venue you're going to be in when you really do make a difference. I think that's an interesting juxtaposition, because we're always talking about business and making money on the net, yet sometimes you have the biggest impact on people not necessarily directly in your own field.

Phil: Impact goes both ways. You can have an impact on someone, but at the same time, they have an impact on you.

Jane: When we first met Ken McArthur, we instantly connected with him. And that's easy to do, because he's so warm and easy-going. Both of us were at the very first jvAlert. But it was the second one, when Ken and Frank and Sterling were on that famous couch, that we started talking about things that really opened a door for Phil and me.

We were running a fairly average, what I would call ho-hum kind of internet business. Ken offered for us to speak at the next jvAlert, and that was a really important offer. He didn't do it because he thought there was money in it coming off of sales at the end. I think he just did it because he thought we were relatively interesting and that we might have something to say to people.

That had a really big impact on our business. We were now speakers at an event. One of our partners came to see us because we were in the area. It lifted up our business recognition.

Phil: Ken is one of those people who is like a big, cuddly teddy bear. He has the most wonderful personality, and it affects everybody who's around him. You can't help but want to get involved in whatever Ken is doing. That always has a rebounding affect on your own business.

Jane: And it's not just Ken there. Since then, Frank Sousa and Phil and I have become friends. We've been on cruises together. We've written a book together. And it all started on that couch. And with Sterling, of course, he interviewed us and we're in the Info Product Blueprint product.

The fact that we were (and still are) in that product got our name known early on. We barged in and got on the couch too. It was a big couch, too, after that, because they accommodated a lot of people. Phil and I are people Ken gave a start to. There isn't anything I wouldn't do for Ken.

I call them the three pillars. Sterling got us involved in his project. We got involved in Ken's projects. Frank got involved in our project and we all did things together.

That's a very important thing I don't think people understand when they do business on the net. They think they can have the greatest product in the world – which they may well have – but if you don't actually go and meet people, and give them a hug or shake their hand or give them a business card or make a real impression, I think it's very tough to have an impact on people.

Phil: One thing I notice and I don't know if it's a gender issue or not, is that women have a unique ability that most men don't have. Ken is one of the rare men who *does* have it. You women have the ability to listen to people and genuinely show you're interested. Most guys don't do that. Most guys will sort of half listen to you.

You'll talk to those marketers at events and they're only half listening because they're trying to get what they want. They're really not paying attention at all. Ken has this talent to genuinely be interested in someone and truly show that interest when he's with you. That's how you have a genuine impact on people.

Jane: It really is the relationships that matter. I'll tell you a funny story about Frank Sousa and me. We'll battle all the time politically. I'll tell him he's crazy. He'll tell me I'm crazy. And yet there isn't anything I wouldn't do for Frank, either. We are the best of friends. We do lots of business together. We think totally differently about the world. And we still love each other.

I would never know that if I hadn't spent hours with Frank as well. People need to get out into the world and meet the people that they're doing business with. If you don't have that connection, it's very hard to have any impact at all. Or if you do, it's very minor.

Without Ken, Sterling and Frank, whom I call the three stools, because they're the underpinnings of our business, our business would be nowhere. Oh, maybe we'd be making a comfortable living online, but maybe not. We are in a whole different stratum that they helped us enter into.

Phil: They're probably responsible for at least two-thirds more business.

Jane: Mike Filsame did a seminar called the Seven Figure Code a few years ago where he taught people how to be millionaires. We were at that seminar. I got up and told stories about how Ken McArthur helped us get from a six-to a seven-figure business.

Phil: The money is a nice by-product, but the relationships are much, much more important. And I think when someone has the impact they're able to add to you as a person. That's much more valuable from my point of view. It comes from those close associations you form over the years.

Jane: We've had some clients for years, but because we're in an expert level of our business now, the phone is always ringing with people wanting to talk to us and wanting to do joint ventures with us or have us speak and that's very important, because it keeps increasing your circle of influence and knowledge.

Because of JV partners, you have a ripple effect. You meet people you never even knew existed though them. Phil probably won't say this, but I will. We do a lot of helping much smaller marketers get a kick-start with their business as well. We don't do it with seminars like Ken does. WE do it through spending time with them on the phone or in person.

Or we do it through MeetUps. We met three people at MeetUps in New York for four or five hours. We really got to know them and got to help them. We had more fun at that dinner than we can at big seminars. They were teaching us things we never heard of, too.

Phil: You learn as much from them as they learn from you.

Jane: We've done 60 or 70 sites on our own, but when we founded SoKule and now its relatives, we had something that was in direct synch with what Ken does in a way that none of our other sites did. When we want to kick around a new idea or new project, Ken is one of the first people we sit down with. It really pays off – not just in money, but certainly in relationships.

You can't do joint ventures successfully unless you have at least an abiding trust with someone, or preferably a solid friendship. If you're not close to people and you can't change directions when needed, then you're going to have a problem with your business. Even when you're more successful, you have to have your ear tuned to your JV partners, so if you're going over the cliff, they stop you! I'm not fond of going over cliffs.

 You just need to have funk, like people, and be at least a little outgoing. Liking people is the key to success. If you don't like people, you better find a different kind of work!

It all started with those key people and over the last ten years it has grown into quite an empire. We're very proud of it. And Ken has been involved every step of the way, and if that's not impact, I don't know what is!

Phil: What many sites lack is what we have with SoKule and our other sites. We WANT our members to succeed, because when they do well, so do we.

Jane Mark and Phil Basten have been helping people succeed on the net for the past ten years. They joined forces and launched their Australian company, JPE Advertising, which was a highly profitable endeavor in its first year. They have developed some of the most innovative websites and scripts on the net including a list building management system, various advertising scripts, and some of the most effective targeted advertising services on the web.

Their latest endeavor, Sokule, was born in 2009 and was created to meet the advertising needs of the internet business community by helping to increase the advertising reach of its members and advertiser.

 Phil Basten is the marketing consultant for JAM Marketing Inc. He is also part owner of JPE Advertising, and is the developer of Sokule.

A good friend once described him as having more ideas than a dog has fleas. He took this as a compliment. Phil is an innovative, insightful, product generating, marketing machine. His focus is developing products and services that work online. His favorite phrase is. "We develop the marketing tools others copy."

Phil has extensive knowledge in counseling, sales training, and the advertising industry. He is a charter member of the Australian Institute of Professional Counselors and has a lot of marketing experience. He was involved in the advertising agency industry in Australia for more than 25 years, working for such prestigious companies as Ogilvy & Mather, Fortune Advertising, and Leo Burnett as a concept creator/ copywriter. His contemporaries dubbed him the "Ad-Man".

Jane is a pocket dynamo who has a typical New York attitude. "Don't tell me how hard it is or how much effort it will take.. get it done."

She ran a multi-million dollar real estate partnership called JED Management Corp. Jane started her own successful catering business in the heart of New York City's Central Park. You guessed, it was called "Jane's".

Like Phil, she has extensive knowledge of people's needs and behavior patterns, having received her master's degree in psychology from the New School for Social Research in New York, and a BA from Brandeis University in Massachusetts. This training, and her business background, have given Jane a unique perspective into both doing business on the internet and discovering what people want by asking the right kinds of questions.

Jane is the author of 4 successful ebooks, *All Your Lists In One Place*, *Joe? Yes, Mabel? Are We Rich Yet?*, *The Magic Bullet*, and the definitive *Guide to Sokule - Sokule - It's Not Your Grandmother's Social Media Site*. Jane takes care of JV Partnerships and marketing. She writes the creative ads that gives the business its zing!

You will often find her on the phone with clients offering marketing tips or delving into the support desk to give a personal touch to Client queries. She is all hands on deck all the time. To Jane every client, large or small, is treated as a VIP. You can find them both at sokule.com.

# Chapter 16

## "Systems"

*No Impact without Clarity*
By Roseanna Leaton

I was lucky enough to come across hypnosis whilst in my teenage years. Like many others, I initially wondered as to its authenticity. You see, I was first introduced to hypnosis in the form of a stage show. Also like many others, I experienced a reaction of both fascination and a little fear.

I would probably have walked away from that theatre still ignorant of the true value of hypnosis had I not been fortunate enough to meet with the hypnotist, Ronricco, and his wife in person. In meeting them I benefitted from the opportunity to discover what hypnosis really is, its validity, how it works and a little of its scope.

This in itself demonstrates two key factors in the story of impact creation.

1. Everything that we do, see, say or indeed think creates an impact, the extent of which can be absolutely huge. The same event can be experienced by different individuals in totally opposite ways.

Many people, I am sure, left that theatre after the hypnotic show with a closed, fearful, or skeptical mind. Others left, I am equally sure, feeling that their life had been transformed with the new possibilities that the state of hypnosis opened up for them.

2. The impact that you experience is greater when you feel a personal connection with whatever it is. In my case, being lucky enough to spend time with a very talented and experienced hypnotist opened my eyes to a new world.

1. Every Thought You Have Creates An Impact...*and hypnosis enables you to choose better thoughts.*

If my very first client had not let me know how pleased they were with their stop smoking session, would I have felt as confident or been as enthusiastic about my business? Would I have seen as many clients? Would I have even come to realize the massive power of the human psyche and the endless benefits of hypnosis? Would my clients' lives have been the same, or very different?

It is very difficult to trace back to whence something began because of the infinite twists and turns, possibilities and choices that one faces on their journey through life. Which individual element had the most impact will always be unclear, although to me there is one overriding factor that underpins almost everything else.

Your (most often unconscious) thoughts and expectations are the power behind the choices that you make. These expectations act like glue as they gather together collections of experiences that accord with them. When they are not playing the part of glue they moonlight as an ultra-strong magnet, attracting new experiences that are then presented as yet more choices and opportunities in your life.

It is difficult to identify the individual parts of the learning curve of life. To me, being a hypnotherapist is so amazingly rewarding. To be able to help another person to see something from a different angle, and to watch them as they grasp their power is so fulfilling. The impact is like a snowball gathering snow as it rolls ever faster down a hillside.

It is difficult for most people to comprehend the scope and reach of hypnosis. Hypnosis is now a mainstream area of neurophysiology research and many excellent, peer reviewed publications support it as a natural state of mind that allows access to your subconsciousness. This is the part of your mind where *automatic and instinctive thoughts* and behaviors are stored.

The brain wave patterns seen during hypnosis have shown researchers that hypnosis decouples cognitive control from conflict monitoring processes of the frontal lobe of the brain (1). That is, it can be used to unlink, re-link, or exchange emotions that have become associated with specific memories stored in the brain. You unconsciously draw from these stored mental-emotional relationships every moment of the day, and also during the night when you dream.

Every single thing you do will involve an unconscious interaction with this part of your mind. Thus, the reach of hypnosis extends infinitesimally out into every large or small area of your life. If there is anything you want to change in terms of instinctive thought patterns, behaviors, reactions or habits, hypnosis has the power to help.

Hypnosis can be used to change your expectations, and therefore change your experience of things. Your instinctive thoughts in turn create your automatic emotional and experiential reactions.

We have yet to discover quite how far hypnosis can reach. The growing body of scientific medical research demonstrates that you can control pain and undergo major operations using hypno-anesthesia (2), overcome fears and phobias and successfully treat PTSD (3,4), lose weight (5), achieve powerful self-confidence (6), play better golf (7) and overcome driving test nerves with the help of hypnosis. These are just a few examples that demonstrate a fraction of the *impact* that hypnosis can have in your life.

Perhaps now you can begin to appreciate why I get so excited about hypnosis? Yet still, I know that you cannot really see the point I am making because for anything to have a true or real impact you have to connect with it personally. You have to feel it and to experience it for yourself.

To really understand what hypnosis is, how it works or what it can do for you, you have to experience it in person.

2. For Real Impact To Be Created, You Must Feel A Personal Connection

A thought without emotion has no real impact. As you read what I have written above you may have agreed (or disagreed) intellectually and logically with my views. But until you *feel* it, there will be no lasting impact. (That's why I provide a free hypnosis MP3 download on my website – http://www.RoseannaLeaton.com.)

Equally important to remember is that a thought combined with the wrong emotion will create the wrong impact.

I am sure many potential marketers will be reading this book in the hope of gleaning tips upon the best ways in which to become successful. Many of you will be third party affiliate marketers, selling (or trying to sell) products created by other people.

The first and most vital tip I would give to you is that if you wish to make a real impact upon others by means of successfully selling products to them you have to truly believe in what you are selling.

You too have to feel a personal connection with the product and fully appreciate its value and worth.

You have to be willing to buy the product yourself, use it and then in turn believe in it. If you do not do this your lack of genuineness and lack of belief will *unconsciously show* in what you say, write and do, either in person or over the Internet.

This might seem obvious. But I can assure you that only one in one hundred would-be affiliate marketers truly accord with this essential key, and only that percentage are usually at all successful. You would be totally astounded if I told you how many potential affiliates have signed up on my website to sell my products without having first bought or used them; and that includes the free one! I hasten to add that this does not apply to all of our affiliates; we have some very genuine end users of our MP3 downloads who have gone on to become invaluable affiliates.

How can these people possibly believe in what they are selling? How can they understand the product? How can they identify with it? How can they in turn instill trust in their target audience? They cannot. It is as simple as that. And this will show in many ways, both conscious and unconscious.

I mentioned before that a thought without emotion does not make an impact, and that a thought with the wrong emotion creates the wrong impact. If your intent is to make money in spite of the product, you are connecting with the wrong emotion and will make the wrong impact, or no impact at all.

If, on the other hand, you are numbered among the professional and ethical people who would truly like to make a big impact for the right reasons, because you truly believe in a product and its value, then your impact will be unlimited.

Think for a moment about Steve Jobs. You might have read his biography. What made him so successful was not simply a desire to make money. That goal was a poor second to his primary and passionate desire to produce amazing products that would transform people's lives. What an amazing impact he has made on the way in which we live our lives.

Do you think he would have tolerated staff working in his sales outlets who did not know about every detail of the products, or did not use them and passionately believe in them?

In a similar way, do you think that I could have run a clinical hypnotherapy business for 20 years almost exclusively reliant upon word of mouth referrals had I not been passionate about hypnosis and a true believer in its impact?

Because I had this experience I wanted to reach out further and help more people to become as excited as I am about the power and potential impact of hypnosis. The fact that medical research had shown in a meta-study (2) that a hypnosis recording can be equally effective as an individual session with a hypnotherapist paved the way to making my goals possible.

## How To Create More Of An Impact Via The Internet

If the Internet had not "happened" and brilliant minds had not come up with all the technology that enables mp3 downloads, I would not be doing what I am doing today. The ever-expanding potential impact of this type of technology has enabled me to transform the way in which I work, and hugely increase the potential scope in terms of people worldwide whom I can help to touch with hypnosis.

I got really excited when I read Ken's book, *Impact: How to Get Noticed, Motivate Millions and Make a Difference in a Noisy World*, as it not only confirmed to me something that I had come to conclude myself, but it gave me an idea of a how I needed to proceed if I wanted to make a bigger impact.

You see, I had come to the conclusion that no matter how good a product or how wide a range of products I had to offer, if nobody noticed them in the noisy world of the Internet they would not help the people I wanted to reach. I had also discovered that I myself did not have either the time or the relevant experience to get noticed on the Web.

I had been extremely naïve in thinking that any IT person/web person could just get us to a great position on Google and that would be it! Everyone would see the products, understand them and use them. How wrong could I have been?

I quickly learned that to work out what terms were relevant and to stay at #1 on Google takes a lot of effort. I also learned that even if you did get to #1 on Google for a specific search term, this in itself did not necessarily translate into sales.

The solution that Ken's book offered to me was so obviously great that I felt myself fizzing with excitement. What I needed was to connect with joint venture partners (or affiliates) who could personally spread the word to their circle of contacts, in a similar way that I had obtained my client base in clinical hypnotherapy for 20 years.

*Word of mouth is always going to be the best way in which to make a real impact.*

I soon discovered that although this principle holds true, there are some provisos. These I have already mentioned. Whether on or off the Internet, to spread the right word you have to feel the right emotion. Joint venture partners have to totally buy into the product themselves. They have to be true and genuine believers or the people they try to reach out to will consciously or unconsciously not trust them.

The need to be genuine is even more essential on the Internet, if that is possible. People are more cautious when they cannot see you or touch you in person. They start out from a skeptical stance. They are aware that the distance and screens that the Internet provides opens the door more readily to being conned. They have to **REALLY** trust you or they will not take that next step to try your product.

The ongoing impact for me in this process is getting involved in this project with Ken, to further refine and define my search for this type of venture partner. I want to make a real, true and genuine impact in this noisy world of ours. And to do this in a bigger way I need to connect with more genuine, like-minded people who wish to spread the word about hypnosis, and also have a skill set that includes sales and marketing.

------------------------------------

With a degree in psychology and numerous qualifications in hypnotherapy, Neuro-Linguistic Programming (NLP) and sports psychology, Roseanna Leaton is one of the leading practitioners of self-improvement.

Roseanna spent 20 years in private practice as Principal Hypnotherapist at the Analytical Hypnotherapy Centre of the Isle of Man. She is listed on the Hypnotherapist Register in the UK and is a member of the International Association of Pure Hypnoanalysts.

It has been the study of the human mind and behavior, along with an innate understanding of the power of thought transference, that has led to thousands of people successfully improving their lives through Roseanna's self help hypnosis mp3 downloads.

Roseanna has written over 450 published articles, and been translated into over 20 different languages. She is a regular contributor to eminent magazines and specialist publications. The communication of her expertise and experiences is much sought after.

A keen 9-handicap golfer, Roseanna combined her knowledge of the game and the mind mechanism to create the acclaimed Golfer Within recordings which enable any player to lower their handicap. This is one of many mental skills 'toolkits' available from http://www.RoseannaLeaton.com.

## References

(1) Egner T, Jamieson G, Gruzelier Hypnosis decouples cognitive control from conflict monitoring processes of the frontal lobe. *J Neuroimage,* 2005; 27(4):969-978.

(2) Montgomery GH, David D, Winkel G, Silverstein JH and Bovbjerg DH. The effectiveness of adjunctive hypnosis with surgical patients: A meta-analysis. *Anesthesia and Analgesia*, 2002;94, 1639-1645.

(3) Butler L, Duran RE, Jasiukaitis P, Koopman C and Spiegel D. Hypnotizability and traumatic experience: a diathesis-stress model of dissociative symptomatology. *Am J Psychiatry,* 1996;153(7 Suppl): 42-63.

(4) Kingsbury S J. Hypnosis in the treatment of posttraumatic stress disorder: An isomorphic intervention. *American J. of Clinical Hypnosis*, 1988;31: 81-90.

(5) Allison DB, and Faith MS. Hypnosis as an adjunct to cognitive-behavioral psychotherapy for obesity: A meta-analytic reappraisal. *J. of Consulting and Clinical Psychology,* 1996;64:513 -516.

(6) Pekala, RJ, Maurer R., Kumar, VK, Elliott, NC, Masten, E, Moon, E, Salinger, M. Self-hypnosis relapse prevention training with chronic drug/alcohol users: effects on self-esteem, affect, and relapse. *American Journal of Clinical Hypnosis* 2004;46:281-297

(7) Pates J, Oliver R, and Maynard I. The Effects of Hypnosis on Flow States and Golf-Putting Performance . *J. Applied Sport Psychology*, 2001;13: 341–354.

# Chapter 17

## "The Mental Criteria Necessary for Success"

*"How to train your mind for success:*
*The Thread of Persistence and Integrity"*
By Curtis Graham, M.D.

*"The characteristic that tends to distinguish the winners from the losers is the relentless conversion of problems to opportunities, negatives to positives." – Dan S. Kennedy, Marketing Strategist*

Do you have an open mind? Can you survive outside your comfort zone?

The story about my success is not about the usual description and running timeline of my life as I lived it. Nor is it about the nearly impossible odds I had to overcome on the way to success. Go to my websites to get that background.

These are popular means of providing examples of how anyone can overcome almost anything they set their mind to do. Critical lessons about success to be learned are found in the motivating and inspirational constituents that give power to your self-esteem (belief in your personal capability to do what it takes), not in methods or examples. These examples are what I want to share with you.

Success is a level of accomplishment that establishes for that individual the degree of satisfaction, fulfillment, and happiness they expect and plan for. Your heart is full and your mind is at peace. When I finally realized that success means something totally different to everyone, the thought that it is unrelated to our physical accomplishments, our actions and our social status presented me with an introspective conclusion that success is the result of what Lee Milteer, motivational speaker, calls "An Inside Job."

Once you begin reading about what other highly successful people attribute their success to, it drives the truth of that fact into your brain.

Early in life we all have imaginative thoughts about what we want to do in our lives, which gives us the first spark for lighting the fire that illuminates the possibilities.

At the time, we don't know it, but we do sense something in our minds that's important for some reason. That spark inevitably incites a course of events that push us into decision making, especially while in high school.

During those early vulnerable years, self-esteem develops. It's not only the influences of parents, family, friends, teachers, religion, and society that smack you in the face all at once. It is the time when you develop what you think about yourself that is added to what people you respect tell you about yourself.

It's a time when you begin to know you have what it takes to make the grade. It's a time when you make a personal decision between doing something worthwhile in life and accepting what circumstances provide for you.

I continued to think about becoming a doctor following my emergency surgery for a ruptured appendix at six years of age. Complications kept me in the hospital another two weeks when I got a taste of what doctors do for patients. Like so many of us visualizing our future early on, we suddenly are impacted by an experience that magically triggers our previously unrecognized and subconscious arena of skills and talents that were there all along.

My school grades had been good, but I had no idea during my teenage years that I had the brains or motivation to do all that was needed to become a physician.

By the time you start college you put yourself to the test. Do I truly want a career in medicine or not? What happens if I find out I don't have the skills and brains I thought I had? Fear of failure and the emotional consequences if you do seem overwhelming at times.

At this time, you usually have a goal in mind, you believe you can make it, and you experience the evidence that your belief in yourself is right.

Visualizing the future for yourself produces inspiration and motivation by powering up your mind to enable it. This happens subconsciously. Your good self-esteem and faith in yourself, as well as your capabilities, propels you even more.

In 1960 Dr. Maxwell Maltz wrote an outstanding book, *Psycho-cybernetics*, in which he revealed his studies about how our minds work. He describes the servomechanism in the brain, which drives you to success, or to failure. The way your brain decides is based on what you have been feeding your brain with over the years of your life.

Brain feeding begins when the umbilical cord is cut and continues 24/7 until you die. Every day of your life, from second to second, is recorded through your senses on into your brain memory banks.

Billions of fragments of information are sent to the brain daily and kept in the subconscious region. So, if you are involved in negative thinking, having bad friends, plummeting your brain with bad thoughts and ideas, the conscious mind hears that and steers you to failure. When you feed you mind with good stuff persistently, then your conscious mind automatically shifts into success mode.

To emphasize this point, every highly successful person I have ever met will testify to the impact this widely accepted mental process has had on their life. Wise people attach themselves to successful people, learn from them, apply their success systems, and insure they are constantly feeding their brain with success nutrients.

It's the quickest, easiest, and most effective path to success anyone can have. That's what I did – unknowingly – for many years of my life.

A few years ago I discovered what I had been doing unconsciously all along. That doesn't mean you can't grab access to that knowledge and belief early in life, say by 14 to 20 years old, and use it from then on.

The problem is no one tells you about it early enough to get the best use out of the strategy. If you don't, or can't believe this concept, you're a loser without even having to work at it.

**Essentials for success:**

*1. College Education Isn't Needed:*

Relying on a college education to succeed is the most abusive propaganda ever publicized. A college education can be a detriment or blessing, depending on the path you choose as a career.

If you want to become a doctor, you are required to have a college education, have good grades, have great recommendations, and be personable.

Many of the multi-millionaires I have met are plain folks like you and me, many of whom barely finished high school.
Dan Kennedy (world renowned marketing strategist), Bill Bartmann (Billionaire—bad debt collections), Ron LeGrand (Real Estate investor), and thousands of others who started in poverty, came from the wrong side of the tracks, and had no idea what they eventually were capable of doing with their lives.

College education has its disadvantages, in addition to being outrageously expensive for the most part. The education you receive has a very strong tendency to instill in you a mindset, which closes your mind to other opportunities and beliefs. One obvious example of this is many students raised in a Bible reading family become atheists during college.

With a closed mind you will intentionally disregard productive time-proven opportunities for success, not recognize opportunities when they appear, and hinders your decision to grab the opportunity before it disappears. Opportunities are always transient.

*2. Entrepreneurial Mind:*

An entrepreneurial mind and attitude is one of the most important factors in you becoming successful. I was lucky in having a grandfather who had been a teacher for 22 years and instilled in my mind the necessity of making myself available to every opportunity to get ahead. I lived with my grandparents on their small 105 acre farm during my teen years. I learned the value of integrity, the value of keeping my word, a hard work ethic without complaining, and old fashioned honesty in dealing with others.

An entrepreneur is a calculated risk taker in a sense. Entrepreneurs have a keen sense of trends, future opportunities, need for continuous self-education, recognizing decisions that have profitability potential, and a profound belief in their own capabilities for solving problems with any barrier that shows up.

Other aspects of entrepreneurs that I highly regard are their unending persistence towards goals, regarding failure simply as a stepping-stone to success and an inherent desire to make a difference in the world.

After retiring from a very successful medical practice in 1999, I had a good amount of time to reflect on my career and life. I discovered that I had been an entrepreneur all my life, and never thought of myself being in that category.

Every physician is a true entrepreneur by doing what they did to reach their career goal. It certainly wasn't by instinct. My mind had to have picked up the entrepreneurial spirit from farm life and my grandfather.

You become your own boss, work for yourself, and take on every task as a challenge, which can (not maybe) be managed in one way or another.

There is always a person, incident, epiphany, or event that occurs in your life, which locks on your brain like a pit bulldog, and provides the eternal inspiration and motivation for succeeding by making a difference in your life. Positive brain feeding is the fuel for that engine.

### 3. Early Business or Career Exposure:

Another essential that holds the key to becoming a success in any business or career is exposure to the realities of both at a very early age.

Repeatedly I read reports in the media of teenagers who start businesses which earn them thousands of dollars a month. Can thousands of other kids in their teen years be encouraged, taught, and supported in those efforts? Absolutely.

I would predict that at least 30% of selected kids would do well and become successful in a business or career at a young age, and never need to waste time going to college, at least until after they become wealthy.

How many times have you heard reports about educated or uneducated people early in their lives drifting around from job to job, place to place and paycheck to paycheck having no direction in mind?

After years of this wasting time spent haphazardly, it's not unusual for them to suddenly lock on to something they have stumbled into and become millionaires soon after, at age 21 (ex. Mark Zuckerberg—Facebook), or 55, or even 80 years old.

Are you aware that 27 of the Forbes 400 Billionaires have only a high school education?

The first key related to exposure that I see is to become aware of your talents and skills early in life (below age 20). Then, by using those attributes you can select a career choice highly likely to succeed for you.

This can happen anytime in your life, but hopefully before age 20, or soon after. The choice must match your talents and skills. You will know what those are by then because you've been using each talent or skill for many years already.

The point here is to make a choice of a career or business early, go for it full blast, and change horses later if need be. The idea is to —take action, gain momentum, keep the brain active and creative, and don't slow down. Those factors can also be easily transferred to any other career if you decide to change careers. It's a lot easier to do when you're still young. When you jump into this process at an older age, it's slower, harder and more of a challenge, but still attainable.

The second key related to exposure is starting your own business, even if you fail. The average successful person has failed in a business or career effort at least three times before they reach real success.

Because most successes stem from a business entity of one type or another (even a medical practice business), the earlier you are exposed to business principles and marketing strategies, the greater will be the probability of a higher level of success over time.

My exposure to what I considered to be an enviable success in my specialty medical practice as I judge it today is laughable—not having the slightest idea of what my capabilities were.

*4. Knowledge about Business Principles:*

It may seem incredible to you to know that medical doctors are taught absolutely nothing about running a business (called medical practice) or about marketing a business.

Of the 142 or so medical schools in the USA, not a single one teaches or advocates learning business principles—you were just expected to know it. The same is true in dentistry and other professions. It means that every physician who starts a medical practice, in foundational business terms, is doing so with absolutely no basic knowledge of how to make their medical practice business successful, let alone how to take it to its maximum earning potential. Might this be a significant factor causing the flood of physician attrition today?

The result is that physicians eventually settle for a mediocre medical practice business for three reasons. First, they don't know what they don't know. Second, they have been traditionally brainwashed during their medical education into believing that if you build it, patients will come storming through your office door. Meaning, there is no need to learn about business principles and the value of marketing, because it all works out magically by itself without that knowledge and education.

Now you can understand why doctors are commonly accused of being poor business people.

Third, physicians don't consider medical practice a real business. Read Michael Gerber's book, —*The E-Myth: Physician*, to understand this disgraceful educational neglect.

You may have noticed the numerous comments in the media about a shortage of doctors. The great percentage of that shortage is because medical practices are failing in droves financially all over this country.

Increasing outside threats to medical practice frustrates doctors, who then quit practice early, retire early, change professions, work harder and burn out, and move into an employee position somewhere.

In addition, these doctors have no idea what they could do to rescue their practices, due to the absence of business education and knowledge. By implementing sound business principles and systems into their practice business, they would survive, grow their business, and reach their maximum potential.

If you expand this belief to all the other careers and professions existing under the same deceptions, it reaches incredible levels of highly destructive effects on our way of life. The saving grace here is anyone can learn and apply such knowledge without a college education.

The problem is recognizing the necessity of doing it.

It wasn't until I had gained expertise in marketing that I recognized that I probably left a million dollars on the table in my career because of never knowing these critical things.
If I had known what I know now, I would still be practicing. I would be at the maximum potential for income and service to my patients.

What I considered as success for me in my medical practice, I now consider less than mediocre—for all of the above reasons.

*5. Ability to Dispel Risk, Inertia and Fear:*

These three success-destroying elements follow you around like a shadow. They often pin you against the wall in order to keep you from stepping out of your —comfort zone.

We all have that envelope around us. It's what you do about it that counts. We live and do things within our own established invisible boundaries where we feel comfortable, secure, and content. Forcing ourselves out of the box we put ourselves in, is not easy. It requires a strong sense of faith in our self.

When I started my private medical practice, it took a threat to my personal practice code and ethics to push me out of my comfort zone.

I was ordered by the chief of the OBG service at the Kaiser Permanente Hospital to either stop spending too much time with my infertility patients, or leave. I left. The issue was not my medical competence. The issue was money. My time with my patients kept my nurse overtime every night which cost the clinic money. I had a major battle with my comfort zone after that, I can tell you.

Among the many fears we need to overcome in order to move outside our comfort zone, the most powerful one is—fear of failure. It exists because we don't credit ourselves with having the capabilities to succeed.

The sad part is we have no idea what we are capable of doing in our lives, so we find our comfort zone and stay there.

Lesson – you must continually push the edge all the time to reach your highest level of success. It means learning to tolerate the insecure area outside your comfort zone for the rest of your life, or career. Your ultimate success is guaranteed to be waiting for you outside your comfort zone. Believe it, or accept a life career of —It's "good enough" even if it sucks. Regrets never fade away.

What to me was such a blistering revelation was that some "extraordinary things" happen when you step out of your comfort zone. Your mind and thinking suddenly become very creative. It's almost automatic, like a switch has been turned on.

Survival mode creates a very similar brain reaction. You find that your mind is quicker, sharper, much more creative, and enables you to do unbelievable things, which you never thought you could do.

How the above issues enabled my practice success:

I'm not speaking about financial success here because I don't consider I had much success in that part of my medical practice business. The success I want to share with you now is about what I accomplished in my medical practice that took me to the top of my expertise in medical care in my specialty, and way beyond my greatest expectations.

The sequence of events that followed the starting of my private OBG medical practice began with my continued interest in infertility work.

Over the first three years in my private medical practice I had developed both a reputation and expertise in infertility that most other doctors avoided doing. Much of the infertility practice procedures weren't covered by health insurance plans in the 1970's.

I expanded my expertise in microsurgery repair of oviducts using delicate ENT instruments. The plastic surgeons refused to let any gynecological surgeon wreck their delicate instruments.

The surgical procedures I learned to do were rarely done in the USA. I had no one else to teach me. Talk to me about malpractice risk and putting myself out on a limb!

About three years later the first tuboplasty and microsurgery courses were developed and taught what I was already doing.

Next came the new surgical use of the laparoscope. It was developed in Germany by Dr. Kurt Semm. Being able to perform major surgical procedures through a 3/4 inch opening in the abdominal wall was an incredible advancement. My associate and I were the first medical doctors in our area to obtain the training with the laparoscope and took the first class ever given in the United States by Dr. Kurt Semm himself.

We returned to our local hospital, requested laparoscopic surgical privileges, and asked the hospital to buy the equipment needed. We were told 'no' to everything. We bought the instruments and equipment needed ourselves, which solved one problem.

After repeated confrontations with the hospital committee about granting privileges, they (the surgical committee made up of other kinds of surgeons and doctors) agreed to supervise us carefully for a dozen or so cases before we would be approved for those procedures. Normally to get privileges approved, a surgeon has to be supervised by another surgeon who is experienced with the procedure.

The irony was that the supervising surgeons didn't have a clue about using a laparoscope or about what could be done with it safely. At the time, few if any surgeons in our country were experienced in using the laparoscope.

We trained the operating room nurses and did the cases without incident. No one on the west coast had used a laparoscope. My associate and I agreed to supervise each other as there was no alternative. At this time we were the only two physicians in northern California with privileges in laparoscopy. Interestingly, it took a couple years after that before the general surgeons in the US thought using a laparoscope was a good idea.

My associate and I continued to expand the number of procedures done with the laparoscope and taught the other gynecological doctors as well (1980's). It eliminated many of those surgical procedures we used to do through a long incision in the abdomen and saved the patients several days stay in the hospital. The surgical technique avoided a prolonged recovery period at home, and no sutures to be removed.

We succeeded because of our persistence, confidence in our own skills and capabilities, and accepting training far beyond the normal and acceptable surgical procedures.

My associate and I had reached the top of our professional surgical capabilities at the time. The shame of it is with the use of sound business knowledge and principles we could have reached much higher levels of practice success financially and professionally.

Small procedures done with the laparoscope later evolved into major gynecological operative procedures.

The first outpatient (done in an outpatient surgery center and was home in 3 hours) laparoscopic assisted vaginal hysterectomy in northern California was done by me successfully with God's help and without complications.

Once the laboratory became available for in-vitro fertilization, I then did IVF for a few years in my infertility practice. It became necessary to stop IVF because of turf battles between hospitals and physicians.

**Comments:**

Permit me to reveal the success factors, which made my professional career the best it could be. These factors are applicable to any business, profession, career, and endeavor you will ever choose to pursue.

1. Mindset—visualization of your goals, open to opportunities, belief in yourself and your capabilities, willing to accept failure as being a stimulus to try again, continual education, persistence, creativeness, overcoming fear and insecurity.

2. Taking action—decision to step out of your comfort zone and willingness to take the risks involved, believing you are far more capable than you first thought, understanding that your mind moves into overdrive only when you are outside your comfort zone, and rarely happens inside your comfort zone.

3. Relationships—treat everyone you meet as if they were a long lost friend, have respect for anyone you deal with, be willing to give without expecting or demanding anything in return, keep your word always, remain fair and honest, and maintain your integrity at every turn, treat yourself as if you deserve what you have worked for, make time for your family and personal life a priority while doing all the rest.

I believe every person is born with a divine assigned purpose, maybe more than one. You will recognize it sooner or later. The purpose may not be the one you thought it was. Looking closely at what happens then, will usually demonstrate to you that you may have started on the wrong track, but you are headed in the right direction.

The lesson is not to try to find your real purpose in life, it will find you. Spend your life in the pursuit of your primary interests and goals no matter what it takes. In doing that, you are automatically shown the right path to follow. You know that because you feel it. You never have to ask yourself, "Is this what I want to be doing for the rest of my life?" You will notice that a warm satisfying feeling comes over you when you are helping others along the way. Actually, that's just part of the success process—making life better for others. John 15:7

"When dealing with people remember you are not dealing with creatures of logic, but with creatures of emotion, creatures bristling with prejudice and motivated by pride and vanity"
---Dale Carnegie

Curt Graham is a physician entrepreneur, widely published in the fields of medicine, business, and marketing while doing consulting, coaching, copywriting, speaking, and teaching.

You can contact Dr. Graham at cgmdrx@gmail.com or marketingAMedicalPractice.com.

# Chapter 18

## "Growth"

*How to grow with your audience*

Bored with retirement, John McLaughlin tried something different. Along the way, he discovered a key principle of impact.

I've been a consultant / coach for over 30 years.

I found retirement boring, so I took up day trading NASDAQ stocks on a whim.

Paper trading felt great and I was soon doing very well. After awhile, I began to take losses, at times big losses. Surprisingly, not according to plan, that's for sure, I was losing more than winning. Emotionally, I would get so upset with myself and the markets that by the end of the trading day I was exhausted and felt like a loser, not what I was at all used to in my life.

Eventually, I stopped trading and switched hats. Off with my loser's hat, on with my tried and true winner's (consultant) hat. I consulted myself. After analyzing the system, I could clearly see what was really going on now.

I needed to think differently, plan and strategize differently, and execute altogether differently. I had to reinvent myself and my system for trading to become a winner again. I had to reinvent my entire game

Winning is all about learning. And learning does not occur, nor will it ever occur, on your own.

# Chapter 19

## "Paying Your Way"

*How to finance your dreams*

I know it's not fashionable, but yes I do really want your money.

I want your money so I can:

- Give real value in return
- Feed and provide security for my family
- Make a difference in the world.

Without money it gets tougher to do that.

Without money you often …

- Focus on survival
- Think about yourself
- Cut corners in what you give

Worst case without money you …

- Lose your self
- Lose your values
- Lose your health
- Die

So why do we apologize for wanting money?

Asking someone to give value in return for value does wonderful things for everyone.

Here's the number one reason we apologize for wanting money.

It's the fear that we aren't really giving value in exchange.

And what's the cure for that?

Give more value!

Co-author Ronda Del Boccio says this about money, mindset, and giving value:

Most of us have received a lot of messages about money that get us messed up in the head. Maybe you've heard that money is the root of all evil, that desiring money is bad, that sales is smarmy, that money doesn't grow on trees, that making money is hard, or any similar message.

The story about how John Di Lemme opened Frank Sousa's eyes to the tremendous power for good that having money can give you is a great reminder to everyone. Let the money flow to you and through you.

Every human being is valuable beyond measure. That comes as part of being born onto this earth. Having money doesn't change your value as a human being. But having it does make a lot of things easier.

My observation is that a lot of people feel innately unworthy and un-valuable.

You ARE worthy and you ARE valuable. Period. You are a bright shining light. You have something valuable to contribute.

I LOVE what Ken said about giving more value.

What does giving more value mean to you?

Adding value doesn't mean adding 10 more pages to the ebook, another hour to the webinar or more "stuff" to the package. Adding value is all about giving the receiver of the value what will help them most - whether that is a customer of your product, a receiver of your service, or simply the clerk who's taking your money at the gas station.

As you focus your attention on adding more value, consider this.

Giving more time or a bigger bundle doesn't necessarily mean you're giving more value.

A one-hour class that teaches all the steps is better than three rambling hours. One page with a clear set of steps is better than 100 pages with no path to follow. A few minutes of focused mentoring that get to the heart of the matter quickly are better than hundreds of aimless minutes.

To a gas station clerk who's been treated like a non-person all day, looking her in the eyes and saying hello can be everything. To the person who buys your product, more value can be giving a shortcut or easy to follow steps instead of a big huge thing with no direction. To someone investing in a service, making sure they get your full attention (not a distracted you) as you provide the service can make a huge difference.

Give tremendous value.

# Chapter 20

## "The 'What Can I Get' Level"

*Most people are stuck*
*– even if this doesn't apply to you*

Of all the people who go to any church, synagogue, temple, mosque, community meeting, political organization or special interest group, most of them are stuck at the "What can I get" level of participation.

In church, most people come looking for that good feeling they get when they see their friends or hear a well preached sermon or see their kids up in front of the church singing. In fact, people start getting upset if they don't get that feeling every time.

Maybe the preacher has a bad day, your friends didn't show up or your kid didn't get picked for the big part in the pageant.

Then you start thinking, "Why do I bother? Is this really worth it?"

A lot of people stop being involved at this stage.

Maybe it's a political party that you thought you jelled with. There was a charismatic politician who you loved to listen to, core beliefs that you felt good about and you thought you could make a difference.

Then the politician got caught in a messy love affair, the party changed its direction and you didn't feel like you even had a voice.

Most people who join a political party are stuck right there.

But a few people go a little farther.

It starts by asking the simple question, "What should I do?"

167

Those people are far more likely to stick around.

If you want people to stick around in a church or a political party, the first thing you should do is give them something to do.

Actions involve us in a way that glues us to a group. It's no longer us versus them. Actions make people into strong, connected, impact producing teams.

But if you really want success, start asking the question …

What Can I Give?

Whether it's a church, synagogue, temple, mosque, community meeting, political organization, special interest group or success with your business, the real rewards come from giving.

If you are asking what you can get, you may in fact get many things.

But if you are giving without anticipation of getting anything back, you will have countless rewards.

When's the last time you really committed to give?

Time and money is short for everyone, and it's easy to stay at the "What Can I Get?" level of participation.

I've done it many times myself, but every time I stay at that level the return on my investment is small.

How much did you commit to the last free e-book you purchased to take your business to the next level?

Let's ramp up the level of participation!

The original jvAlert membership system was great partners who put out quality joint venture offers to the best of the best.

But what if we really ramped that up? That's what the new Impact Partnering Program is all about.

http://theimpactfactor.com/impact.htm

I want to actively DO things together, because learning is great, but doing is what makes success happen.

Have you noticed?

All through my life, I've been DOING things, not just talking about it.

And I've learned …

We can do so much more doing things together than if we try to do it all by ourselves.

If your life needs to change, there is no better time than today to get started on the rest of your life. Check out what we are doing today.

http://theimpactfactor.com/impact.htm

# Chapter 21

## "The Five Stages of Change"

It's time for you to make a change because if you don't, the world is just going to change things for you, without your having any say at all.

Lots of people have heard of the five stages of grief, but did you know there are five stages of change?

Psychologists Carlo DiClemente, PhD, and James O. Prochaska, PhD, identified five stages of change, in a study on smoking habits. The stages that they identified include *precontemplation, contemplation, preparation, action, and maintenance.*

Guess what! The same stages are involved when you try to move your impact to the next level.

In *precontemplation* you aren't even thinking about changing, so let's ignore that stage for now.

Once you get to the *contemplation* stage, you are most likely to respond to feedback and education as sources of information about growing your impact. Then in the *preparation* stage, you commit yourself to changing and seeking a plan of action.

If you are in the *action* or *maintenance* stages, you are actively changing your behaviors and environments.

That's where the researchers found that social reinforcers were most important.

Then there are the relapsers who cycle back into earlier stages. Yes, it's true we DON'T always move forward in a straight line climb to the top!

So where are you, and what can you do to really change the results of your business, your actions and your life?

If you are unaware, wake up! Start reading, looking and learning.

If you are contemplating making a change, continue your education and start moving into action.

Meet people who are doing what you are doing and start with a first step.

If you are taking action, keep it going!

Small steps that are COMPLETED make a huge difference at this stage!

Also, remember the importance of social reinforcers to your success. Everyone needs support. That's why live events like JV Alert Live are so important to your success!

If you are actively moving and taking massive action all the way to completion, this reinforcement becomes even more important so that you don't lose the momentum that you have built up. It's easy to be distracted or discouraged, so use other people to keep you on track and moving forward at full speed. Other people can be inspiring!

If you backslide, then regroup, and start where you are. Don't get discouraged when you fall back a stage. It's a natural part of the growth curves that we all face. Perspective can be a very useful thing, so look around you and discover who else has experienced what you are going through right now.

# Chapter 22

## "Something Has To Give"

It's become painfully evident to me – I can't do everything I need to do – something has to give. The question is what do I give up, and who gets hurt by it. Disappointing someone doesn't feel good.

I always think I don't really need much.

When I met my wife, I was renting what was supposed to be an office in a condo building. It had a single room which measured about 10 feet square with a bathroom attached.

I slept on an old orange couch — not a hide-a-bed, but almost long enough to curl up on with my 6'4″ frame with my toes sticking out the end under the armrest.

I'd walk down to the grocery store and buy a bag of bagels and just munch on a bagel when I felt hungry.

It was a simple life, and no one was demanding anything from me. I had enough money to pay the bills and pay for a bit of time in a recording studio to work on my music.

I was making about $200 a week. It was a simple, good life.

When I got married, things got a little more complicated. 31 years later life is still good, but it's not as simple.

I could still live in that office, eat bagels and live a simple life; and to be honest, it sounds pretty good sometimes. But to do that, I'd have to give up a lot.

First of all, I'm pretty sure my wife doesn't want to live in a 10 foot square office and sleep on a small couch – certainly not with me in it, too.

Then there's the son in college – college bills up the ante a bit. So the simple gets a bit more complicated when other people start to get involved. It turns out people have expectations of you.

- Your parents want to see you succeed.
- Your spouse wants to be loved and supported.
- Your children want to be cared for.
- Your business partners want your focus.
- Your friends want your time and attention.
- Your customers want results.

It turns out that people all have needs, and if they are connected with you they have needs, wants and desires they hope YOU will meet.

Ironically, the more successful you are, the more people need and want you. And you want to help.

This can pile up.

I can't imagine what it must be like for someone who is really famous or really wealthy. So many people must want something from them. It's frightening.

You don't have to be famous or wealthy to be overwhelmed by the needs of others. I know you've felt it too. As much as we love giving to others, and as much as we may generate energy from giving passion and purpose, eventually we realize we only have so much to give.

There are only so many resources and so many hours.

Maybe you've been a volunteer for a religious or civic group.

If so you probably realize, once you volunteer and actually do something for someone, the number of people who ask you to volunteer seems to grow exponentially. There's always a need for reliable volunteers.

Or maybe you are a natural leader.

If you are even a semi-public figure, the number of people who want you to help solve their problems increases dramatically. If you really think about it, you know we are pretty demanding of our leaders.

I've been building relationships online since there first was an online.

Over the last 15 years, there have been literally hundreds of thousands of people who have been directly connected to me in many, many ways.

They come and go, some closer than others, and they all have needs.

At this instant, I'm probably in recent contact with 40 to 60 thousand people who in one way or another are looking for me to help them.

Some of those needs are more urgent than others.

I have good friends dying of cancer, in danger of losing their homes, and battling through divorce right now.

I have literally thousands of people who are friends or subscribers who can't pay their bills this month. And I only have so much to give them.

I know deep in my heart, the best things to give are those small moments of encouragement you give when someone is beaten down.

Those are moments that have real impact.

But words only go so far.

That's where action comes in. It's not so much that you "feel" someone's pain. It matters more when you "do" something about it.

Right now, I have too many projects and not enough time and resources.

Cutting any of my projects will hurt someone.

Think of it ...

- Should I quit doing my live events?
- Should I stop writing?
- Stop working with non-profits?
- Ignore my kids?

If something has to give, there are lots of choices to make.

- You can try to be more efficient with your time.
- You can focus on projects producing results.
- You can try to get more resources.
- You can outsource tasks other people can do better.
- You can beg, borrow or steal.
- Or you can do nothing.

If you do nothing, chances are things won't get better, and most likely will get worse.

That's what usually happens when we just get tired and decide to quit — not always, but usually.

So what am I going to do?

Here are my six steps out of overwhelm:

- Breathe
- Relax
- Think
- Act
- Evaluate
- Repeat

If you keep taking these steps, you will have a real impact.

Most of what I'm doing is here:

http://theimpactfactor.com/impact.htm

# Chapter 23

## "The Pareto Principle"

**The Pareto Principle** (also known as the 80-20 rule, the law of the vital few, and the principle of factor sparsity) states that for many events, roughly 80% of the effects come from 20% of the causes.

It's been widely applied – with gleeful ignorance in many cases – to almost anything in life.

At its core, it seems to indicate that you should concentrate more of your resources on the things that work for you, and less on the things that don't.

Here are some very common things that don't work.

- Trying to please everyone
- Trying to help everyone
- Trying to fix everyone
- Trying to do everything
- Trying to know everything
- Trying to be everything

Yes, I'm going to ask you to put a little skin into anything you do, but it's nothing that you can't afford if you really see the value in what we can do together.

I have a lot of ways I can help people, so here's what I've decided to do:

I'm going to …

- Please people who want to be pleased
- Help people who want to be helped.

- Fix people who want to be fixed.
- Do what is effective.
- Know what is needed.
- Be the best I can.

I hope you will be too!

Sheila Taylor's business allows her to work from home, travel and more. Here is what she said about her life:

> "My business allows me to travel, be my own boss, and spend time with family and friends when I desire. I've been with a few businesses in the past and never liked what I was doing. I also worked in the corporate world for about 10 years and hated it!
>
> I now have a wonderful fiancé that I've been with for 7 years. I am also a mother of 2 girls and 1 boy, and a grandmother of 2 boys that I love just as much as my own children. I now live the lifestyle I've always dreamed of and I'm very happy. I owe it all to my business, my fiancé, & God, for standing by my side and supporting me through everything. I love traveling, meeting new people, and making new friends.
>
> My favorite saying is "You're Never Too Old to Start Something New". The reason I say this is because no matter how old you are, you are never too old to start living the good life and having exactly what you want out of life!"

Here is what Ronda Del Boccio says about focusing on the Pareto Principle:

When you think about making a difference in a measurable way, there is no way to predict how what any single person does will spread. But what you can do is pick a certain area in which you desire to create an impact and focus your attention on that.

It is too common to fracture your focus and scatter your energies. Anyone who wants to leave the world a little better than they found it is likely to be attracted to any cause, movement or medium that exists to create a positive change. Beyond Gandhi's remonstration to be the change you want to see in the world, I add this: Choose a focus.

You're not approaching the idea of making a difference from a perspective of expecting to get something back or to get "brownie points," and everyone only has so much time and energy.

Just like any other area of life, zooming in on one or two areas – focusing on that 20 per cent of your efforts - will bring about 80 per cent of your results. This is a great way to streamline your time and energy in any aspect of life.

So rather than scattering your time, energy, and attention to a hundred worthy causes, focus on one or two things that are nearest and dearest to your heart. Use any skills you have along with your passion in order to "amp up" your message. Work from your strengths.

One easy focus for anyone is to treat people well. Ellen Degeneres ends her show by saying, "Be kind to one another." That is simply a matter of attention and self mastery. Perhaps that will be one area you choose to focus your own attention.

That alone will cause a million smiles or more.

True, kindness or love or the effect of a smile is not something you can easily measure (with current technology), but it is focus that does not require any specific training, situation, or money.

Since you only have so much time and energy – so many resources – narrow your focus and exponentially increase your effectiveness!

# Chapter 24

## "Life is Hard, Then You Die"

*"Life is hard. Then you die. Then they throw dirt in your face. Then the worms eat you. Be grateful it happens in that order".*
— David Gerrold

So Why Don't You Just Give Up!

When I was 32 years old, I was considered a loser.

I'd been striving to be a rock star on the hard streets of Hollywood, working whatever job I could find to support my wife and two young daughters, but no doubt about it, the future didn't seem all that secure.

The theme was, "Why can't you be a success?" and a secondary theme was, "Why don't you go back to school so you can get a real job?"

And the truth was, I'd done a lot of things without a huge amount of measurable success. Pretty much I'd been doing all the things that were interesting and creative and fun and not worrying too much about how I was going to support a family now and in the future.

So my wife convinced me to go back to college.

And I decided — against her better judgment — if I was going to go back to college, I was going to major in music.

Just for the record, that's not the optimal route to supporting a wife and family, but that's what I decided.

So I started back to school …

But there were problems!

First of all, I played a little guitar (not very well) but that was it. Zero piano skills, didn't play another instrument.

I could sing, but I was a bass/baritone and couldn't tell you the notes on the bass clef.

What can I say, I was fearless.

I was a bit out of place.

First of all, most people starting college for a music degree are 18 years old, not 32.

I had a wife, two young daughters, a full-time job and a couple part-time ones and was carrying a double load of courses.

I was also in a hurry.

The day that I started, a brand-new music professor led the choral program. He was fresh from receiving his — still wet from the press — doctorate at the University of Oklahoma and as far as we understood, he seemed to think he knew everything in the world about choral music.

And he wasn't afraid to let you know.

Setting himself up as head drill sergeant, he plowed through the ranks of the choral department like a tank, leaving bodies everywhere.

He intended to raise the standards of the choral program and make a mark for himself in record time.

Proudly displayed on his T-Shirt was the saying ...

"Life is hard. Then you die."

At first I was convinced that he was determined to make everyone's life very hard and then possibly to kill them off one by one, but then my perspective changed a bit and I discovered that he was a lot like me.

He was a little scared, I think.

This was his first big position and he needed to be outstanding. He was trying to do that very hard.

Along the way he alienated big chunks of the staff and students, but he learned quickly a little humility can go a long way.

Eventually we both relaxed enough to breathe.

And I found him to be amazingly supportive of me and my Quixotic efforts to learn something about music.

For as long as I was willing to try, he was willing to support me — all I had to do was keep trying.

That wouldn't have been true of everyone. Dr. Belan was amazing at taking me exactly where I was — with zero skills — and moving me to a higher plain.

Eventually, I finished a 4 year degree in two years, by really scrambling, and then went on to a graduate degree studying with Dr. Belan, but it wasn't easy.

Along the way Dr. William Belan was an amazing support to me. He challenged me every step of the way, and showed me that perseverance and quality are valuable beyond measure.

Thank you Dr. Belan.

Dr. Belan has been teaching choral music for over 30 years at California State University, Los Angeles and directs one of largest choral conducting graduate degree programs in the United States.

He's a pretty amazing man.

So many times along the way, I could have quit in an instant.

I think it was partially my desire not to let Dr. Belan down after all of his support that kept me going through 6 years of studying when it wasn't easy to juggle the jobs, the family and the kids, along with getting my degrees.

Today I got requests for help from two desperate people.

They are both living in situations with seemingly hopeless prospects.

They believe they will not be able to make it without my help, or at the very least, they want me to take their pain away.

Of over 60,000 people who are members of my sites, come to my live events or subscribe to my newsletters, many of them are going through terrible times.

There's a 10% chance of awful things happening to you this weekend.

For any given weekend, I project that 10% of all of the people have something major go wrong in their lives, such as the loss of a loved one, divorce, loss of job, serious accident, etc.

The list goes on.

That means in my family that 6,000 people are having a major problem right now.

And I want to help.

Maybe the t-shirt has it right. "Life is Hard. Then We Die."

Life is certainly hard at times.

But even if it were true, what good does it do to give up?

What can the world gain if you stop short of your goals?

Albert Einstein did not speak until he was four years old and did not read until he was seven. His parents thought he was "sub-normal," and one of his teachers described him as "mentally slow, unsociable, and adrift forever in foolish dreams." He was expelled from school and was refused admittance to the Zurich Polytechnic School.

Charles Darwin gave up a medical career and was told by his father, "You care for nothing but shooting, dogs and rat catching." In his autobiography, Darwin wrote, "I was considered by all my masters and my father, a very ordinary boy, rather below the common standard of intellect."

Henry Ford failed and went broke five times before he succeeded.

F. W. Woolworth was not allowed to wait on customers when he worked in a dry goods store because his boss said "he didn't have enough sense."

Walt Disney was fired by a newspaper editor because "he lacked imagination and had no good ideas." He went bankrupt several times before he built Disneyland. In fact, the proposed park was rejected by the city of Anaheim on the grounds that it would only attract riffraff.

You know the list goes on.

Do you want to quit 3 feet from the gold?

# Chapter 25

## "Life is an Adventure"

Life is a challenging and wonderful adventure. I'm so curious about what the possibilities are, and so eager to learn whatever truth there is.

I admit – just as Solomon said long ago – "This is chasing the wind."

Life is beyond my comprehension and I know it, but it doesn't keep me from trying.

I think about the vastness of space or the tiny universes that we are made up of, how atoms connect or electrons or quarks. Life is infinitely big and infinitely small, and I can't comprehend either extreme.

And so in my adventure, my life is always full to the bursting point.

There is never room for one more thing until I kick something else out, because I've packed my life as full as it can handle.

The universe is so large and I am so small and I have so much I want to explore.

Every moment of every day, I am forced to decide where my time and focus will be spent, because there is not enough time in history to contain the things that I want to know, or the adventures I want to experience.

It's not a quest for the adoration of the masses driving me.

Crowds are fickle and quickly leave their heroes. Today's heroes are easily forgotten and torn down.

It's not the truth that drives me.

There is no final answer that I'm looking for. Wisdom is fleeting and knowledge is ever changing.

So what is the purpose of this adventure? What will make my life fulfilled?

I've looked at what makes people happy and have come to the conclusion; we are most blessed, most fulfilled and most satisfied when we are giving freely without guilt, duty, expectation, or obligation.

In giving, we have value.

So what do I have to give of real value?

Every person has real value.

In my life I've been a singer, composer, recording engineer, writer, speaker, teacher, programmer, salesperson, marketer, entrepreneur, coach and volunteer. The labels for my life could go on for hours.

- I've had jobs that were menial and I've been in positions to inspire thousands.
- I've been thought worthless and I've been praised by many.
- I've been ignorant and I've taught and coached Harvard PhDs, millionaires and "household names."

But none of that is my real value.

My real value is the same value that every person has – certainly that YOU have – to make someone's life a little better.

It doesn't always take something big. In fact, it usually takes something small.

Small actions change the world.

So what about small actions changing my life?

I've had so many wonderful adventures in my life; where did that all go?

What about all of the things that I'm missing?

People spend a lot of time thinking about what they are missing.

Doesn't it make me sad to know how much I've lost?

Not really.

Sure I miss some of the things that I've done, the people I've lost touch with, the places I've been, but my life isn't devoid of things I've had before, it's crammed with new things I'm living in this instant.

- If I don't spend my time with music, it's only because there is so much more out there to experience.
- If my love life is not what it used to be, there is no lack of excitement to come in the future.
- Life is not sad at all — It's a choice.

Should I fill my life with regrets, lost opportunities and fears?

Not for me, because there is enough adventure in the world to last a thousand lifetimes and I have no more space to fit everything wonderful in.

Like it or not … You make a difference!

# Chapter 26

## "Now it's up to YOU!"

Sad but true, most people who read this will be too late, because one of the hardest things to do in life is to decide.

I don't know about you, but I tend to agonize over decisions.

I spend 90% of my time …

- analyzing
- appraising
- brooding
- cogitating
- conceiving
- considering
- deducing
- deliberating
- estimating
- evaluating
- examining
- figuring out
- imagining
- intellectualizing
- judging
- meditating
- mulling
- pondering
- rationalizing
- reasoning
- reflecting

- ruminating
- studying
- weighing
- worrying

And then hopefully at some point I make a decision.

Often … much too late.

When what I really should have done was actually DO something.

All the way to completion!

In all of the time I spent doing everything in the list above, I could have actually made a decision, taken an action, and have the results.

The results might not have been perfect, but at least I have results to work with.

REAL Results!

When you take action all the way to completion, you see what really happens, not what someone predicted would happen.

And …

You are one step closer to where you want to be.

If you are still struggling and confused about all of your options for making an impact, stop and make a decision, because if you don't …

It will be too late.

Most people will keep analyzing, appraising, brooding, cogitating, conceiving, considering, deducing, deliberating, estimating, evaluating, examining, figuring out, imagining, intellectualizing, judging, meditating, mulling, pondering, rationalizing, reasoning, reflecting, ruminating, studying, weighing, worrying.

YOU, on the other hand, can be MILES ahead.

I hope that you will join us in working together to have a bigger impact. Check out our Impact Partnering Program today.

http://theimpactfactor.com/impact.htm

The Impact Factor: How Small Actions Change the World

# The Sequel:

## "The Impact Manifesto"

- You make a difference, whether you want to or not.
- If you do nothing things get worse, so take positive actions to make things better.
- Build up instead of tearing down, because your smallest actions have the greatest impact,
- Your mindsets, knowledge and skills combine with the actions you complete to make a difference.
- Leverage the art, science, technology, strategies and tactics of creating massive impact for remarkable results.
- Your mind, body and spirit must be at their best to create maximum impact.
- You can do so much more working with others than you can alone.
- Build long-term relationships to create long-term impact.
- Be active in giving communities to sustain you when life is hard, and increase your impact to infinity.
- Your impact WILL grow beyond one life.

Take it to heart and put it into action.

# Acknowledgements

This book was a long time coming. There were many days I thought that it would never get to completion and it's a testament to the help, support, patience and encouragement of many people that it finally is.

This book is the result of literally four years of constant research, reflection, and writing. It would not exist without the help of countless people.

Without the crucial encouragement and occasional swift kick to keep me moving from my beautiful wife of almost 32 years, Roxanne, I would never finish a book, so ultimately she is due the credit for everything in this book and so much more.

Special thanks go out to Ronda Del Boccio who assisted with interviews and the writing of this book and my special co-author contributors, Phil Basten, Dr. Curtis Graham, MD, Roseanna Leaton BSc (hons) (Psych), LLB, dhp, MIAPH, Jane Mark, Michael Savoie and Cheri Sigmon.

The always amazing Seth Godin gave generously of his time to support this project by giving me an interview for the book at a time when this book was just a glint in the eye of the future. I don't value that time lightly, because as the best-selling author of *Linchpin, Tribes, The Dip, All Marketers are Liars, The Purple Cow* and so many other bestsellers and as the most influential business blogger in the world and as the founder and CEO of Squidoo.com and as a very popular speaker, Seth's time is priceless.

My special thanks go to Anita Cohen-Williams for proofing this manuscript and doing an amazing custom, professional index for the book, to Mike and Carolyn Lewis for constant support and help with the book layout and publishing and to Michelle Alvarez for all she does to make my life outstanding.

My wonderful children, Angela, Melissa, and Stephan, are constant examples of the way we impact thousands every day. I'm impressed and proud every day by the ways they grow and flourish, and proud always to be their father.

.My parents, Irvin and Margaret McArthur, ingrained in every cell of my body that there are no limits on what we can do when we serve others and live it by example. My siblings, Jean, Robert, and John have been a constant loving, supporting, and inspiring factor in my life since the day they were born—despite the fact that they STILL believe that I tried to hang at least one of them in my youth.

My mentors and friends are endless, and I'm terrified if I mention any of them that I'll leave out the most important.

I'm surrounded by the love and support of the amazing community of friends—the members of The Impact Partnering Program (TheImpactFactor.com), The jvAlert Live Family (jvAlertLive.com), the speakers, expert panelists, and attendees at all of the jvAlert Live and "One Day Intensive" (OneDayIntensive.com) events; and the subscribers of my blog (KenMcArthur.com) and newsletter—have made achieving my dreams possible.

Thank You!!

# About The Authors

## Ken McArthur

Ken McArthur, best-selling author of *Impact: How to Get Noticed, Motivate Millions and Make a Difference in a Noisy World*, has enabled thousands of people to achieve amazing impact by championing the philosophy that partnerships and collaboration build value for everyone.

Ken challenges us to realize we ALL have an impact – whether we want to or not – on thousands of people who we touch in our day-to-day lives by demonstrating that simple things make a HUGE difference.

The popular host of a series of live events that bring together top-level marketers, entrepreneurs, business owners, corporations and non-profit organizations to create multi-million dollar joint venture relationships – he creates incredible, intense impact for product launches and multi-million dollar profits in surprisingly short timeframes.

Regularly asked to speak at leading marketing events, he has managed product launches ranked in the top 400 sites on the Internet. Ken McArthur is also the creator of AffiliateShowcase.com, a pioneering affiliate program search engine and directory system and the founder of the MBS Internet Research Center, which conducted the world's largest survey ever attempted on the subject of creating and launching successful information products.

Not satisfied to concentrate entirely on large organizations, Ken also works with select individuals to help them create a decent living utilizing the power of the Internet.

Ken was the official mentor for Sterling Valentine as he took his launch from ZERO to over $100,000 in less than 8 days. Ken and Sterling documented the process as a "proof of concept" for Info Product Blueprint, a massive home study course that is the "bible" of info product creation.

Ken offers top-level coaching and mentoring programs designed to help individuals, corporations and non-profit organizations reach masses of people using the techniques, tactics, strategies, and systems that he has developed specifically to help people spread their ideas, products and services around the globe.

# Ronda Del Boccio

Ronda Del Boccio unknowingly began her path to becoming "The Story Lady" as a tot when she invented skits and stories with her stuffed toys. She was born with eye conditions that mean she will never drive or see "normally," so she lives every day with added challenges that she calls "speed bumps." Now she lives in the country.

All her life people have opened up to her and shared their lives in the safe space she innately offers. Recognized globally as "The Story Lady", she teaches authors, business owners, entrepreneurs, and visionary individuals just like you to reach your ideal customers, readers, and associates through the power of your story.

Along with Bonnie Tesh, she co-authored the inspirational book "I'll Push You Steer: The Definitive Guide to Stumbling Through Life with Blinders On". Her new books "The Peace Seed", "The Instant VIP", and "The Geometry of Success" come out soon. She is an award-winning author, transformational speaker and mentor who teaches authors and entrepreneurs how to connect with anyone through the power of storytelling, and live from your power.

She is a globally published, award-winning author who LOVES to speak to groups and teach people to bring their best into the world.

# Resources

For additional resources and detailed information on the subjects covered in this book, visit the Impact Factor Resource Center at http:TheImpactFactor.com/resources/.

This resource center offers hundreds of hours of free resources in multiple formats from some of the top marketing experts in the world.

Here are some resources to get you started now:

Ken McArthur's Blog
http://KenMcArthur.com

The Impact Factor – Mentoring, Coaching and Partnering Programs
http://TheImpactFactor.com/coaching

jvAlert Live Events
http://jvAlertLive.com

One Day Intensive Events
http://OneDayIntensive.com

Affiliate Showcase – Affiliate Marketing
http://AffiliateShowcase.com

Market Research
http://mbsinternet.net

Product Creation
http://InfoProductBlueprint.com

Ken McArthur's Help Desk
http://MyHelpButton.com

Ken McArthur's Books
http://kenmcarthur.com/books/

Ken McArthur Speaking
http://kenmcarthur.com/speaking/

Ken McArthur Events
http://kenmcarthur.com/events/

Ken McArthur Media Requests
http://kenmcarthur.com/press/

# ~Name Index~

Bacak, Matt, 119
Bagnall, Brian, 119
Bartmann, Bill, 149
Basten, Phil, 125-33
Bechtold, Alan, 119
Belan, William, 184-86
Boyce, Sanyika Calloway, 70
Burchard, Brendon, 70, 71, 82, 85, 90
Butts, Rick, 95-96

Capps, Ron, 70
Chaney, James, 126
Comm, Joel, 80
Cunningham, Court, 119

Daniels, Jim, 37
Darwin, Charles, 187
Del Boccio, Ronda, 78, 79, 164-65, 180-82
Descartes, Rene, 23
DiClemente, Carlo, 171
Di Lemme, John, 49, 164
Disney, Walt, 187
Dr. Mani, *See* Sivasubramanian, Mani

Einstein, Albert, 187

Filsame, Mike, 130
Ford, Henry, 187

Garon, Frank, 38
Gerber, Michael, 153
Godin, Seth, 15-19
Goodman, Andrew, 126, 127
Graham, Curtis, 145-60
Grudzinski, Miro, 85-93

Hale, Stephanie J., 119

Jenkins, Andy, 36
Joyner, Mark, 119

Kahneman, Daniel, 54-55
Kennedy, Dan S., 145, 149
Klemmer, Brian, 119
Koenigs, Mike, 46, 47, 51, 110
Kosmin, Joelle, 123-24

Leaton, Roseanna, 135-43
LeGrand, Ron, 149
Lorenz, Ed, 29-32, 33, 34, 35; Lorenz attractors, 33; Lorenz equations, 33
Lovingood, Scott, 119

MacLeod, Hugh, 103, 107-108, 109
Maltz, Maxwell, 147
Manning, Randy, 52
Mark, Jane, 125-33
Mazzullo, Mary, 70
McArthur, Ken, 78, 79-80, 109, 110, 119, 121, 128-30, 131; and Impact Manifesto, 197
McLaughlin, John, 161
Merz, Mike, 38
Millet, Cheryl, 52
Mlodinow, Leonard, 51-52
Moos, Chris, 121

Pachter, Charles, 89, 90
Phillips, Deremiah, 64-66, 67-69, 70, 75
Poincare, Jules Henri, 32-33
Prochaska, James O., 171

Russell, Bertrand, 53

Savoie, Micheal, 73-76

Sayles, Kristi, 119
Schwerner, Michael, 126
Semm, Kurt, 157
Shafran, Joshua, 119
Sigmon, Cheri, 77-84
Sivasubramanian, Mani, 120-21
Slattery, Felicia, 70
Sousa, Frank, 38-39, 41-50, 51, 61, 70, 109-10, 128-30, 164

Taylor, Sheila, 180
Toth, Rob, 119

Valentine, Sterling, 38-39, 128-30

Wellman, Jeff, 62-64
Wellman, Keith, 62
Whitlock, Warren, 70
Wilkerson, Carrie, 81
Woolworth, F.W., 187

www.ingramcontent.com/pod-product-compliance
Lightning Source LLC
Chambersburg PA
CBHW071951090426
42740CB00011B/1895